THE PSALMS FOR CHILDREN

60 Object Lessons on the Psalms
Series A

ELDON WEISHEIT

AUGSBURG Publishing House • Minneapolis

THE PSALMS FOR CHILDREN—SERIES A

Copyright © 1983 Augsburg Publishing House

Library of Congress Catalog Card No. 83-70510
International Standard Book No. 0-8066-2016-1

Scripture quotations are from the Good News Bible (Today's
English Version), 1966, 1971, 1976 by the American Bible So-
ciety and are used by permission.

MANUFACTURED IN THE UNITED STATES OF AMERICA

Contents

Preface

The psalms were written to be sung. Many of the great hymns of the Christian church are psalms set to music. The addition of music to the words of the Scripture adds to the feeling that comes from the written message.

Because the psalms are poems, they cover the wide range of human emotions. The psalms express not only the joy and thankfulness of those who worship God, but also the fear, anger, hope, doubt, love, and other emotions that are a part of our lives. The psalms show us that people who lived long ago felt the same emotions that we feel today. Even more important, those who wrote the psalms show us that these feelings may be brought before the throne of God in worship.

Feeling thankfulness and joy is not in itself an act of worship. The feelings become acts of worship when we recognize God as the source of our joy and as the giver of the blessings that make us thankful.

Our frustrations and our fears can also become part of our worship. When our painful emotions make us stand up to God, to argue with him, to complain to him, to tell him what is going on in our souls, these feelings also bring us to worship a God who listens and cares. As the psalmists pour out their feelings to God, they also show their feelings about him. They know his power and wisdom; they depend on his mercy and grace.

The Old Testament poets already saw in God what has been revealed to us in Jesus Christ. They were not afraid of God. They told God how they felt. They knew he was the only one who could help.

The sermons in this book are based on messages from the psalms applied first to children and secondly through the experience of children to adults. When the psalms are sung, the music helps the hearer remember the message. In these sermons objects are added for the same reason. The message is not in the object. The message is in Jesus Christ who has shared in our human emotions so we may share with him his relationship with his Father, our Creator.

I thank the members and guests of Fountain of Life Lutheran Church for their contribution to these sermons. Their ability to bring the needs of the world into the sanctuary and to take the love of Christ back with them into their daily lives has helped remove the distinction between pulpit and pew—and made these sermons possible. I also thank Mary Lou Schram for being a willing proofreader.

ELDON WEISHEIT

It's Fun to Wait

THE WORD

I was glad when they said to me,
"Let us go to the Lord's house."
And now we are here,
standing inside the gates of Jerusalem!
Psalm 122:1-2 (First Sunday in Advent)

THE WORLD

A Christmas gift with a tag
"Do Not Open Until Christmas"

Have you seen any Christmas presents at your house yet this year? Let's pretend this present has your name on it. Someone might give you a gift this far ahead of Christmas. You would be glad to have the present now. However, look at the sign on the package. It says, "Do Not Open Until Christmas." You have the gift now. But you have to wait until you can open it. You receive the gift twice. Once today, when someone hands it to you. Again, on Christmas day when you open it.

King David talks about receiving a gift twice in our psalm for today. First he says, "I was glad when they said to me, 'Let us go to the Lord's house.'" Notice he was glad. He looked forward to being in God's house. He wanted to be with God and with God's people. He enjoyed planning the trip. It was fun for him to wait for something important to happen.

Then he said, "And now we are here, standing inside the gates of Jerusalem!" The day had arrived at last. He could do what he had planned. He had enjoyed waiting for the big day, because he knew that the day would finally come. That's the same reason you can enjoy receiving a gift today. What if you could never open the package? That would be no fun. It's fun to wait if you know the day will come when you can open it. David enjoyed waiting for the day he would go to the temple, because he knew the day would come. And it did. He went to the temple and enjoyed all the things he had dreamed of.

A long time ago God promised the Jewish people that he would send a Savior to them. He said the Savior would be for all people. The people who believed God's promise enjoyed waiting. They knew God would keep the promise. When the right time came, God kept the promise. Jesus was born. Jesus grew to be the Savior who gave himself as a sacrifice to pay for the sins of the whole world. He also died and rose from the dead to give all of us a life that will never end. For many years people had waited; then Jesus came.

You are now waiting to celebrate Christmas, Jesus' birthday. But we are celebrating what we already have. The package is open. We know he has already died for us. We know he is still alive and with us. We already have the gift of eternal life through Jesus Christ.

But we are also waiting. Jesus has promised to come again in a way that we can see and hear him. He will come to take us to heaven with him. We are like people who have received a wrapped gift like this. We already have Jesus with us, but we are still waiting. But it is fun to wait. We can enjoy waiting because we know Jesus is already with us. On Christmas you can open the gift. Then you can see it and use it, but you already have it now. Jesus is already with us, but we are waiting for him to come so we can see and hear him. It's fun to wait, because we know he will come.

9

Where Will the King Live?

THE WORD

All kings will bow down before him;
all nations will serve him.
He rescues the poor who call to him,
and those who are needy and neglected.
He has pity on the weak and poor;
he saves the lives of those in need.
                    Psalm 72:11-13 (Second Sunday in Advent)

THE WORLD

Pictures (or models) of three homes: a run-down
apartment, a middle-class home, a palace

When a person moves to a new neighborhood, he has
to look for a place to live. Maybe your family has moved
to a new home. If so, you had to find a place to live.
You needed a home near where mom and dad work. You
also needed a home you could afford.

Someone is coming! I'll be a real estate agent and
show you three places where the one who is coming might
live. First this is a run-down apartment in a poor area.
Maybe it costs too much, but it is the cheapest place to
live. Here is a house in a middle-class neighborhood; it
costs more, but it is nice and comfortable. This is a
palace; it is big, beautiful, and very expensive.

Let's find out which house the one who is coming will
live in. The psalm for today says the one coming is a
king. It also says, "All kings will bow down before him;
all nations will serve him." He is not only a king; he is a
King of kings. Kings could live in this beautiful home,
and the king who is coming could afford to live in a
home even greater.

But remember, when looking for a home, a family also wants to be close to its work. Let's see what kind of work the king will do. The reading says, "He rescues the poor who call to him, and those who are needy and neglected. He has pity on the weak and the poor; he saves the lives of those in need." The king who is coming may have the money to pay for a palace, but he does not work there. He works with those who are poor, who are in need, who are neglected. He works here *(point to run-down apartment)*. He came to help those who are hungry, those who need clothing and a better place to live. He needs to be near his work; the king needs to live here.

But he also lives here and here *(point to other homes)*. He lives with people who are in need. Some people need food and clothing; all people need love and mercy. Some need better housing; all need a way to heaven. Some need medical help; all need forgiveness.

This psalm was written long ago. It promised that a king would come. Jesus Christ came to be that king. After he was born, kings came to worship him. Ever since, kings and other great people have bowed down to worship him. But Jesus, who is a king, is also a servant. He was born and lived in poor places. He took care of all people. He fed the hungry and cured the sick. He died on a cross to save sinners.

Jesus the king still lives with us today. When we are in need, he helps us. He also helps us help others. Because he loves us, we are the kings who bow before him and worship him. Because he lives in us, we are the ones who can help others in need.

Get the Right Gift

THE WORD

The Lord sets prisoners free
and gives sight to the blind.
He lifts those who have fallen;
he loves his righteous people.
He protects the strangers who live in our land;
he helps widows and orphans,
but ruins the plans of the wicked.

Psalm 146:7b-9 (Third Sunday in Advent)

THE WORLD

An assortment of wrapped gifts, including a book

Let's pretend these packages are the gifts you are going to give to others this Christmas. You have them all wrapped. The packages look pretty, but they have no names on them. You forgot to put the tags on the gifts. Now you don't know which package is for which person. Does that mean you have to open the gifts and start over?

No, you know what the gifts are. You can tell which is which by looking at the package. Let's think about one gift, for example, and see if you can find it without taking off the wrapping. You bought a book for your father. Can you tell which package is the book?

This package is round. It can't be a book. This one is too small. Books are heavy, and this package does not weigh much. But look at this gift. It's the size of a book. Feel it. It's heavy like a book. Then pinch it right here at the corner. You can feel the cover of a book. Now you know which package is for your father, even though you had no tag on it and you did not open it.

In the same way we can find the most important gift of

Christmas. Christmas has many gifts. Not only do you receive packages, but you also eat special foods, go to parties and family get-togethers. Most important of all, God gives you his Son, Jesus the Savior, who is the gift that makes all the other gifts possible.

But sometimes we lose the most important gift among all the others. We forget what the gift is and why we need it. Remember how we examined each of the packages to find the one that had the book? We can also examine all the fun and excitment of Christmas to find the most important gift. We have to know what we are looking for. The psalm for today gives us the clues. It says, "The Lord sets prisoners free and gives sight to the blind. He lifts those who have fallen; he loves his righteous people. He protects the strangers who live in our land; he helps widows and orphans, but ruins the plans of the wicked."

We found the book because we knew its size, weight, and shape. We can see Jesus when we see what he does. He helps people. He frees those who are in prison. He heals the sick. He gives joy to those who are sad. He forgives all who sin. He welcomes lonely people.

Jesus does all these things by being with us. Christmas is important to us because it tells us God came to live with us. Jesus is here to help us. When you are sad or lonely, when you hurt or feel guilty, look for the gift God gave you. The other gifts won't help then. Only Jesus can forgive sins. Only Jesus can promise to be with you all the time. Only Jesus can give you eternal life. Get the right gift—the one God gives.

Who's at the Door?

THE WORD
Fling wide the gates,
open the ancient doors,
and the great king will come in.
Who is this great king?
He is the Lord, strong and mighty,
the Lord, victorious in battle.

Psalm 24:7-8 (The Fourth Sunday in Advent)

THE WORLD
A cassette tape on which you have recorded a variety
of sounds: doorbells, knocks at doors, and others

Listen to this. *(Play the tape.)* What do you want to do when you hear those sounds? Makes you feel like opening a door, doesn't it? Was there a bell that sounds like your doorbell? Did any of the knocks sound like someone you know?

Now listen to one more sound that tells us someone is at the door. This is not a doorbell or a knock. It is a message from Psalm 24. It says, "Fling wide the gates, open the ancient doors, and the great king will come in."

When people come to visit our home, they knock on the door or ring the doorbell. We welcome them by opening the door. King David wrote this psalm to remind the people of Jerusalem that someone special was coming to visit them. He wanted the people to be excited about the visit. He wanted them to open the city gates and the temple doors so the visitor could come in.

When someone knocks at our door, we wonder who it is. We don't open the door for strangers. The people of Jerusalem were also afraid of people they didn't know.

They would not open the city gates to just anyone who came along. David knew they would ask, "Who is coming?" so he asked and answered the question for them. He said, "Who is this great king? He is the Lord, strong and mighty, the Lord, victorious in battle."

The king coming to Jerusalem was not the leader of an enemy army. Nor was he just another king from the next country dropping by for a visit. The king who was coming to knock on their door was God himself. God was going to visit his people. David told the people to be ready so they could open the door.

Many years later, when Jesus came, some of the people were ready, but many were not. Some heard the message of angels who said Jesus had come, but others were busy or afraid. They didn't hear God knocking on the doors of the world. But Jesus came anyway. He came to be the Savior of the world.

Jesus still comes to be with us today. He still comes to tell us that God lives with us. He still comes to forgive our sins, to love and help us. Christmas is the message that God came to earth to become a person like us. We get ready for Christmas by listening for the sound of Jesus at the door.

Jesus will not knock or ring a bell, but we can listen for sounds that remind us Jesus is coming. When someone says "Merry Christmas," remember that we are happy because we have a Savior. The greeting is like Jesus knocking at your door to say he is with you. Listen to the Christmas songs, the bells, the laughter. Each one is the doorbell that Jesus rings to tell us he has come to be with us.

Something New to Sing About

THE WORD

Sing a new song to the Lord!
Sing to the Lord, all the world!
Sing to the Lord, and praise him!
Proclaim every day the good news that he has saved us.

Psalm 96:1-2 (Christmas Day)

THE WORLD

A dry, moldy sandwich and a fresh one

The psalm for today tells us, "Sing a new song to the Lord! Sing to the Lord, all the world! Sing to the Lord, and praise him!" Not only does it tell us to sing a song of praise to God, but it tells us to sing a *new* song. If you are going to sing a *new* song, you have to have something *new* to sing about.

For example, we sing songs to thank God for the gifts he gives us. Suppose you sang a song of thanks to God for food, and this is the food you got *(show old sandwich)*. It is dry and moldy. If you were really hungry, you would eat it. But this sandwich looks a week old. The song of thanksgiving should have been sung seven days ago—not now. This old moldy sandwich doesn't rate a new song.

Now look at this fresh sandwich. For this you can sing a new song. It is fresh for you today. Think how often you eat fresh food. It may be the same kind of food you had a day or a week before, but it is fresh when you eat it. Because the food is new, you can sing a new song of praise for it.

Today we are celebrating Christmas, the birth of Jesus Christ. The Christmas story is an old story. Most of the songs we sing are old songs. I guess that many of the decorations on our tree at church and on your tree at home are older than you are.

Is the Christmas message like this sandwich *(point to stale one)* or this sandwich *(point to fresh one)*? Do we hear only the same old story and sing the same old songs? Or can we sing a new song?

Listen to the rest of the psalm. It says, "Proclaim every day the good news that he has saved us." The message of Christmas is that Christ came to be our Savior. This psalm was first sung by the priests when David was king. They knew God saved them. Almost a thousand years later Jesus came to be the Savior of the shepherds, the Wise Men, and all who worshiped him then. Now 2000 years later, we still worship him, because he is our Savior today.

Every day we can tell his message: "He has saved us! He has died for our sins. He has given us a new life!"

The old story of Christmas is new for us, because Jesus is still our Savior today. When we sing the old songs, they are new songs, because they tell us that Jesus is with us now. The Christmas story is not like the old, dried sandwich. The message that Christ is our Savior is fresh and new every day, so we can sing a new song to the Lord. We can proclaim every day the good news that he has saved us.

What God Has Done Is Good

THE WORD

How wonderful are the things the Lord does!
All who are delighted with them want to understand
them.
All he does is full of honor and majesty;
his righteousness is eternal.

Psalm 111:2-3 (First Sunday after Christmas)

THE WORLD

A potholder or other gift made by a child and wrapped
as a Christmas present

On the last day of school before vacation Amber came
home with this package. It is the Christmas present she
made for her mother. Her mother was pleased when
Amber brought it home. The mother said, "Thank you for
giving me a gift. You have wrapped it nicely." Then they
put the gift under the tree.

Amber liked to look at the presents under the tree.
She was interested in the ones for her, but she also liked
to look at the one she had made for her mother. Then the
family all came together and opened the presents. Everyone was busy looking at the gifts and saying thank you.
Amber's mother forgot this package. It stayed under the
tree behind some wrapping paper. The next day Amber
was sad because her mother had forgotten the gift. Then
her mother opened the gift *(do it)*. When she saw the
nice gift Amber had made for her, the mother said, "You
not only did a good job wrapping the gift, Amber. You
also did a good job making the gift. Thank you."

God has given you a gift for Christmas. You are reminded of the gift when you see the manger with the

baby Jesus asleep in the hay. We came to worship Jesus on Christmas Eve. We said, "Thank you, God, for giving us such a good gift." When we worship God, we tell him he did a good job. Psalm 111 says it this way, "How wonderful are the things the Lord does! All who are delighted with them want to understand them. All he does is full of honor and majesty; his righteousness is eternal."

The psalm writer praised God for all the good things he did, just as we praise God at Christmas for the wonderful story about Jesus' birth. But the psalm adds another thought. It says that when we are delighted with the wonderful things God has done, we will want to understand them.

Remember Amber's mother and the gift? The mother thanked her for the gift and said the package was beautiful. But Amber was not happy until her mother opened the package and used the gift. The psalm tells us that when we praise God for his gifts we will want to understand those gifts.

We have praised God for the birth of Jesus. God did a good job. Do you understand the baby in the manger? This is the baby who grew up to be the Savior. He is the one who died for our sins and rose from the dead to give us eternal life. Christmas tells us about a gift God gave a long time ago, but we still have the gift today. Jesus is still with us. Soon we will take down our Christmas trees. We will put the gifts and decorations away. But we keep Jesus with us all the time.

The Name for Everyone

THE WORD

O Lord, our Lord,
your greatness is seen in all the world!
Your praise reaches up to the heavens;
it is sung by children and babies.
You are safe and secure from all your enemies;
you stop anyone who opposes you.

Psalm 8:1-2 (The Name of Jesus)

THE WORLD

The following words printed on flash cards: JESUS,
TEACHER, PARENTS, DOCTOR, POLICEMAN

Here are names or titles of some people who help you. This says PARENTS. Think of some of the ways your mother and father help you. Can you tell me some? This word is TEACHER. What is your teacher's name? How does your teacher help you? This word is DOCTOR. Do you know your doctor's name? When do you go to see your doctor? This word is POLICEMAN. Do you know a policeman? When does a policeman help you?

This word is JESUS. When he was eight days old, Mary and Joseph named their baby Jesus. When do you need Jesus? When you are lonely or afraid, he is with you. When you sin, he forgives you. He loves you so you can love other people. He gives you hope, joy, and peace. When you die, he will take you to heaven.

Think of Jesus as one of many people who help you. I can put his name in with the others. You could add more names. But Jesus is different from all the others who help you. You need parents now, because you are a child, but later your parents will not help you in the same way they do now. You have teachers now, but later you may be the one who teaches others. You need a doctor or a policeman only at special times.

All of these helpers are temporary. No one needs them all of the time. We need special friends to help us at special times. But Jesus is for all people at all times.

Listen to how King David described how God helped him. In Psalm 8 he wrote, "O Lord, our Lord, your greatness is seen in all the world! Your praise reaches up to the heavens; it is sung by children and babies. You are safe and secure from all your enemies; you stop anyone who opposes you."

People who are concerned about health need doctors. Students need teachers. Children need parents. But all people need God. God sent Jesus to be the Savior of all people. Even children and babies can worship Jesus. He can help everyone.

I am glad that many people love you and help you. I want to be your friend and help you too. You can also help me. When you love Jesus and give your praise to him, you help me see that Jesus loves me. He is the friend of us all. Mary and Joseph gave their son the name Jesus. We love the name Jesus because he is our Savior.

Strength on the Inside

THE WORD
Praise the Lord, O Jerusalem!
Praise your God, O Zion!
He keeps your gates strong;
he blesses your people.
He keeps your borders safe
and satisfies you with the finest wheat.
Psalm 147:12-14 (Second Sunday after Christmas)

THE WORLD
A glass Christmas tree ornament, an empty cardboard box, a paper bag containing an empty coffee can

---

What do you do with the ornaments from your tree when Christmas is over? *(Take one from a tree or show an ornament.)* Sure, you put them away in a safe place for next year. Do you think I should put this ornament in this sack, or in this box? Which is safer?

Maybe the box would be better. It is stronger. *(Put the ornament in the box.)* But what would happen if someone sat on the box. The box would be mashed and so would the ornament.

The paper sack would not protect it either. Or would it? Look what happens when I press on the sack. See, I cannot mash it. Do you know why? Look, it has a can inside. If I put the ornament in the can and the can in the sack, it will be safe. The box looked stronger, but all its strength is on the outside. The sack had something stronger on the inside.

Are you like the box or the sack? Many things want to mash us. We sin and feel guilty. We get sick or hurt. We may feel lonely and afraid. Those are things that mash us.

22

Sometimes we try to protect ourselves by being like the box. We put all our strength on the outside. We can save ourselves from some problems, but not from all of them. Life can mash us down.

But we don't have to pretend we are strong. We are really like this sack: we can be crushed easily. But God sent Jesus to come into our lives. Jesus is like the can inside the sack. The sack is weak on the outside, but it has a strength on the inside. Now I can't mash it.

Christmas is the story of how God sent Jesus to come into our lives. He came to earth to give us his strength, because he knew we were weak. He knew we would sin, so he paid for our sin. He knew we would die, so he died for us. We celebrate Christmas by praising God because Jesus lives in us.

The psalm for today tells us why we can praise God. It says, "Praise the Lord, O Jerusalem! Praise your God, O Zion! He keeps your gates strong; he blesses your people. He keeps your borders safe and satisfies you with the finest wheat."

Jesus did not come to build a city wall around us like a fortress. He is not a box that gives us strength only on the outside. Instead, Jesus came into our lives. He lives inside the walls with us. We can still feel pain and sorrow, because we are still weak on the outside. We are like the sack: we can be crushed and hurt. But Jesus is with us. We will not be destroyed. He will keep us safe forever.

For this we praise the Lord!

A King of Kings

THE WORD

All kings will bow down before him;
all nations will serve him.

Psalm 72:11 (The Epiphany of Our Lord)

THE WORLD

Four children's games (checkers, Sorry, etc.)—each in
its own box—and a large box to hold the four games

See this game. *(Take a game from the big box and open it.)* It has many pieces. *(Show them.)* If we were to play this game, we would need all the pieces. The box is an important part of the game, because it keeps all of the pieces together. All of the things necessary to play this game are in this box. But here is another game, and all of its pieces are in this box. Here is another—and another.

I showed you these games in boxes to help us understand our reading from the psalm. The psalm talks about kings. Not many countries have kings today. Most nations have presidents or premiers. In some ways they are like kings, because they are leaders of their countries. But at the time the Bible was written, a king had greater power. All the people in his country would bow down to him and serve him.

Think of this box *(show one of the games)* as the king and all the pieces in the box as being the people in his country. The king has authority over the people. He holds them together the way this box keeps the pieces of the game together.

However, each king ruled over only his own country.

The people in other countries did not serve him. They served their own king. We keep the pieces for each game in its own box, just as people served their own king.

Now listen to the psalm about kings. It says, "All kings will bow down before him; all nations will serve him." That sounds strange. People bow to kings; kings do not bow down to others. All nations do not serve the same king; each nation serves its own king.

The psalmist is writing about a special king, the king we know as Jesus. Jesus was not born like a king. His family was poor, but their ancestors had been kings. Jesus was a descendant of King David. Even though Jesus was poor, kings came to worship him and to give him gifts. King Herod tried to kill him, and a Roman governor ordered him to be killed on a cross. But Jesus was king even over death. He rose from the dead, and he still rules in heaven at the right hand of God the Father.

Since Jesus rose from the dead, kings and queens, presidents, premiers, heroes and heroines, and many other great people have bowed down to worship him. People from all nations accept him as their Lord and Savior.

Look at the games again. The box for each game is like the king of a nation. But did you notice that I brought all the boxes in a larger box? This big box holds all the other boxes. Just as each game had a box to keep its pieces together, all of the boxes are kept together in a bigger box.

Jesus is like the big box. He is King of kings. He is also a king for all people. He is your king and my king. Today we worship him just as the psalm said the kings would come to worship him long ago and that people of all nations would bow before him.

Look Whom God Chose

THE WORD

You love what is right and hate what is evil.
That is why God, your God, has chosen you
and has poured out more happiness on you
than on any other king.

Psalm 45:7-8 (First Sunday after the Epiphany)

THE WORLD

A large can of juice, a middle-size can of fruit, a small can of soup—all on a tray

---

If you could choose only one of these *(show tray)*, which would you choose? If you are thirsty, you would want the juice. If you are hungry, you have a choice of fruit or soup. If you want something big, you get the juice. If you want something small you take the soup. Each of you might choose in a different way.

God has chosen you. He loves you and wants to be with you now. He wants to take you to heaven. But how did God choose you?

Our psalm tells us how God made the choice. It says, "You love what is right and hate what is evil. That is why God, your God, has chosen you." God chooses the one who loves good and hates evil. Does that mean he chose you? Let's pretend the big can means you love all good and hate all bad. The little can means you hate all good and love all evil. If God chose that way, he would take the big can.

But maybe you are not like either the big can or the little can. You love good, but do you *always* love *all* good? Do you want to forgive everyone who has hurt you? Love everyone—even your enemies? Help all people who need it? Those are all good things, but maybe you do not always love to do them.

Do you always hate evil? You hate some evil. There are many bad things you do not want to do. But everyone loves some evil. We like to hear about some bad things. We like to think about some bad things. We like to do some bad things.

Does that mean God will not choose you? You are not all good *(point to big can)*, but you are not all bad either *(point to small can)*. I have only one middle-size can here, but there could be many sizes between the big and small. We are like the sizes in between. We love some good and some bad. We hate some evil and some good.

How is God going to make a choice? Will he take only those who are perfect? If he accepts those who do just a little bit wrong, how about those who do a little bit *more* wrong? I'll show you how God chooses. Look at the tray and the three cans. I will pick up only one item and show how God makes his choice. *(Pick up the tray.)*

See, I chose the tray. When I picked up the tray, I picked up only one item—the tray—but I also lifted all three cans. When I choose the tray, I get the cans too.

When the psalm says God chose the one who loves good and hates evil, it is not saying he will choose some people and reject others. He chose Jesus to be our Savior. Jesus hated all evil. He hated it so much that he died to pay for all sin. Jesus loved all good. He loved good so much he gave all of us a new life so we can do good by his power.

We are like the cans. The tray is like Jesus. God chose Jesus, but Jesus died for us and rose again. So when God chose Jesus, he also chose us. God did not chose us because we are perfect. He chose Christ because *he* is perfect. Christ takes us along with him.

What Do You Talk About?

THE WORD

In the assembly of all your people, Lord,
I told the good news that you save us.
You know that I will never stop telling it.
I have not kept the news of salvation to myself;
I have always spoken of your faithfulness and help.
In the assembly of all your people I have not been
silent about your loyalty and constant love.
          Psalm 40:9-10 (Second Sunday after the Epiphany)

THE WORLD

Lunch box, workbook, and trophy

Rachel came home from school carrying these three things *(show lunch box, workbook, and trophy)*. Her mother said, "Hi, Rachel. What did you do at school today?"

Rachel could show this *(lunch box)* and say, "I ate lunch today." Or she could show this *(workbook)* and say, "I did my lessons." Or she could show this *(trophy)* and say, "I won this."

Which would you have talked about? If you had won a trophy because you did well in sports, art, or music, would you talk about your lunch? Would you talk about one of your lessons? I don't think so. We talk about what is most exciting to us. For most of us, winning a trophy is more exciting than lunch or lessons.

King David wrote today's psalm. He did many exciting things. He won battles. He built a city. He killed a lion and a giant. He had important friends and visitors. What do you think he would want to talk about? He forgot all those things and talked about something else. He wrote,

"In the assembly of all your people, Lord, I told the good news that you save us. You know that I will never stop telling it. I have not kept the news of salvation to myself; I have always spoken of your faithfulness and help. In the assembly of all your people I have not been silent about your loyalty and constant love."

When David was together with all the people in the assembly, he did not tell about the great things he had done. He didn't talk about his victories. He didn't talk about the city he had built. He was more excited about what God had done. He told the people that God is faithful and helpful. He said God was loyal and loving. He said God had saved them.

David was like us. We always talk about what is most exciting for us. Think about all the good things that have happened to you. You have many things to talk about, and I like to hear about the things that are important to you. I also like to tell you about the things that are important to me. Something exciting has happened to all of us. Jesus has come to be our Savior. He saves us from sin and death. He is faithful to us and helps us. He loves us. It is exciting to know that God is with us. We want to talk about him and hear about him. We want to tell others, "There is Jesus, who takes away your sin."

Don't Hide from Me, God

THE WORD

Hear me, Lord, when I call to you!
Be merciful and answer me!
When you said, "Come worship me,"
I answered, "I will come, Lord.
Don't hide yourself from me!"
        Psalm 27:7-9a (Third Sunday after the Epiphany)

THE WORLD

A dollar bill and a school textbook

The psalm for today tells us how King David and God talked to each other. David said, "Hear me, Lord, when I call to you! Be merciful and answer me!" David sounded like a child coming home from school. He comes in the house and says, "Mom, where are you? I want something to eat. Can you hear me, mom?" He asks his mother for help at the same time that he asks if she can hear him. David asks for help and mercy and at the same time asks if God can hear him.

Then God answers. He says, "Come worship me." This is an invitation. God tells David to come and enjoy being with him. But David only heard a voice. He had to find God to worship him.

David says, "I will come, Lord. Don't hide yourself from me!" David wanted to worship God, but first he had to find him. Like a child going from room to room looking for his mother, David went looking for God.

You and I can talk to God as David did. We look for him. We say, "Help me, God. Hear me." God says, "Come and worship me." We say, "I will come, Lord. Don't hide yourself from me."

I do not like to think about God hiding from me. Adam and Eve hid from God after they had sinned. God came looking for them. We may try to hide from God when we have done bad things. But God comes to look for us to tell us we are forgiven. If we hide from God, he will find us. But if God should hide from us, we would have no way to find him. If God hid himself from us, we could not find him unless he wanted us to find him. I think he wants us to find him. Let me show you two ways to hide.

First, I will show you how to hide something that you do not want anyone to find. See this dollar? If I wanted to keep the dollar for myself I would hide it where no one could find it. *(Suggest several places in the area.)* If I chose a secret place, no one could find it but me. But suppose I wanted to give you the dollar for your birthday. I would want to surprise you. I might take one of your school books *(show book)* and ask what you are studying. You might tell me that your lesson for tomorrow is on page 33. Then I would hide the dollar between pages 32 and 33. You would carry your book to school without knowing the dollar was there. Then when you opened the book to study your lesson, you would find it. I hid it in a place where I knew you would find it.

God does not hide himself in places where we cannot find him. Instead he hides in places where we need him. Each of us needs special help when we are sick, sad, or afraid. Jesus comes to be in those places to help us.

When you ask God for help, remember how God talked to David. Hear God tell you, "Come worship me." Then remember where God hides himself. He hides where you need him. He is there to help you. If you have sinned and need forgiveness, tell him about your sin and he will be there to forgive you. Tell him where you hurt or why you are afraid, and he will be there.

God will never hide from you to keep away from you. Instead, he will hide in your life where you need him. Then you can always find him.

Find Out What Changes You

THE WORD

Happy are those who reject the advice of evil men,
who do not follow the example of sinners
or join those who have no use for God.
Instead, they find joy in obeying the Law of the Lord,
and they study it day and night.

Psalm 1:1-2 (Fourth Sunday after the Epiphany)

THE WORLD

A cup of green water and another of red water, a pack
of tissues, and a spoon

Sometimes we do, say, and think good things. At other
times we do, say, and think bad things. What makes us
change? Where do the good thoughts and words come
from? Where do the bad ones come from?

Let's find out by looking at these two cups. *(Hold cups
so children cannot see the contents.)* Can you tell what
color is in each cup? If I let you look inside the cups, you
would know. But there's another way to find out. Watch.
(Put one end of a tissue in each cup.) You know that
this cup has green water, and that one red, even though
you have not looked inside the cup. The color in the water
changed the color of the tissue that touched it.

You and I are also changed by the people we are with.
If you are with someone who tells lies and uses bad words,
it will be easy for you to change and be like that person.
You will take on that person's color. If you are with someone who is cruel, or someone who complains, you can become like that person.

The psalm for today tells us to look at the people who
change us. It says, "Happy are those who reject the advice

of evil men, who do not follow the example of sinners or join those who have no use for God." Notice it does not say we are to hate people who do wrong things. We are not better than they are. But we are not to follow their ways. We are not to become like them.

The Psalm says the people who are happy "find joy in obeying the Law of the Lord, and they study it day and night." When we study God's Word, we are with him. We receive his gifts of love, kindness, and peace. We are changed by him to do, think, and say good things.

The psalm makes it sound easy. If we don't let bad people change us to be like them, but if we do let God change us to be like him, we will be happy. But the problem is that we are also sinners. We are not only like the tissue that is changed by the water. We are like the water that changes others. When we do wrong, we can also change others.

But we have help. Jesus came to be with us. Jesus is not like a tissue that changes to the color of the water it touches. He is like this spoon. When the spoon is dipped into the water, it does not change color. Jesus could live with us sinners and not be changed by us. He even took our sin on himself when he died on the cross. But he rose from the dead and is still with us. Instead of letting our sin change him, Jesus let his goodness change us.

I cannot wash out the tissues and make them white again. But Jesus did pay for our sins and make us holy again. Now look at yourself. What changes you? Do some people bring out the worst in you? Do they make you think, say, and do things that make you and others unhappy? Then remember that Jesus came to be with you and also with those who bring out the worst in you. You do not have to be changed by the others. Instead, Jesus can change you and them.

Take Your Own Light with You

THE WORD

Happy is the person who has reverence for the Lord,
who takes pleasure in obeying his commands.
Light shines in the darkness for good men,
for those who are merciful, kind, and just.

Psalm 112:1, 4 (Fifth Sunday after the Epiphany)

THE WORLD

Two flashlights—one that works and one that doesn't

Kevin and Brian belonged to a Boy Scout troop. The troop planned an overnight camping trip. The leader told each of the Scouts to bring his own flashlight. Kevin thought it was dumb to carry a flashlight. He already had a big load of food and a bedroll. Since he knew the leader would check, he took a flashlight *(show the one that doesn't work)* with him.

Brian knew that if the leader told them to bring flashlights, they would need them. He picked up his light and checked to see that it worked. *(Show that the light works.)* That night the Scout leader introduced a game. Each boy was to find as many different kind of tree leaves as possible. The one with the most leaves would win.

Kevin grabbed his flashlight and ran into the woods. However, his light did not work. See, it has no batteries. *(Demonstrate.)* Kevin tried to find leaves in the dark, but he could not tell one kind of tree from another. Brian's light worked, so he was able to find many different kinds of leaves. He won the game.

Brian had done what the Scoutmaster had asked. He knew that if the leader told them to take the flashlight there was a reason for it. Kevin did not want to do what the leader said. He took a flashlight only because he had to. His light did not help him.

This story is a parable about us and God. We are the Scouts. God is the Scoutmaster. God tells us things to do. Do you try to do what God tells you because you want to? Or because you have to? The psalm for today says, "Happy is the person who has reverence for the Lord, who takes pleasure in obeying his commands." We are happy if we do what God tells us because we want to, not because we have to.

God has a reason for telling us what to do: he loves us, and he wants us to have a good life. He wants to help us so much that he not only told us what to do, but he also sent Jesus to be our Savior. Jesus did the good things we cannot do. He died to pay for the bad things we have done. God is on our side. When we know he loves us, we can love him and enjoy doing what he tells us to do.

The psalm also says, "Light shines in the darkness for good men, for those who are merciful, kind, and just." Jesus has been merciful, kind, and just to us. These things are lights he gives us. When we go out into the dark world, we have a light, because we have the love Jesus has given us. We are like Brian, who had batteries in his flashlight. But if we refuse to listen to God, if we do not let him love us, we are like Kevin, who had a light with no batteries.

The psalm tells us the light will go with us into darkness. The light we have is the light of Jesus Christ. It is the mercy, kindness, and justice he has given to us. When we take that light with us, we can see the way even in a dark place. Others will also see his light in us, and they too can have the mercy, kindness, and justice that Jesus gives to all.

How Can We Be Saved from Sin?

THE WORD

How can a young man keep his life pure?
By obeying your commands.
With all my heart I try to serve you;
keep me from disobeying your commandments.
Psalm 119:9-10 (Sixth Sunday after the Epiphany)

THE WORLD

A picture drawn by a child, and a plastic bag

The person who wrote today's psalm was talking to God about a problem. He said, "How can a young man keep his life pure?" I think the man was talking about himself. He wondered how he could avoid doing things that are bad. He had heard others say things that were not good. He had seen others do bad things. So he asks, "How can a young man keep his life pure?" The young man knows the answer; so he gives it. He says, "By obeying your commands." We know he is talking to God, because God has given us the commands we should follow. He asked a question and received an answer. But that doesn't solve his problem. He says, "With all my heart I try to serve you; keep me from disobeying your commandments." He has been trying to obey God's commands, but he also asks God for help. It is not enough that God told him what to do. He also needs God to help him do what he should do.

It works this way. Suppose you drew this picture at school *(hold up child's drawing)*. You wanted to take it home, but it is raining. You know the rain will ruin the picture. You ask the teacher, "How can I take my picture home without getting it wet?" The teacher could say, "Don't get any water on it." That's true: if you don't get any water on it, it won't be wet. But that's your problem, so you ask the teacher to help you keep water off the picture. She gives you this plastic bag. She puts the picture in the bag and ties it shut. Now it won't get wet. The teacher not only told you what to do; she also showed you the way to do it.

God also helps us by telling us what to do, and by giving us a way to do what he tells us. We know God's commandments, but we cannot always do what he tells us to do, and we often do what he tells us not to do. We can try to obey his commandments, but we cannot do it by ourselves. So, like the psalm writer, we ask God for help.

God helped us when he sent his Son Jesus to live with us. Jesus did the things God told us to do. He did not do any of the things God told us not to do. Even though he was the only one who obeyed all of God's commandments, Jesus was punished for sin. He took our punishment. He was like the plastic sack. He got wet, but he kept the picture dry. He was punished, but he kept us from being punished.

The Bible tells us that when we are baptized, we are in Christ. We are like the picture in the bag. Water cannot ruin the picture, because it is in the bag. Sin cannot hurt us because we are in Jesus. God has told you what you should do and what you should not do. He has also helped you obey his commands, because he sent Jesus to be your Savior.

Do You Want What You Deserve?

THE WORD

The Lord is merciful and loving,
slow to become angry and full of constant love.
He does not punish us as we deserve
or repay us for our sins and wrongs.
    Psalm 103:8, 10 (Seventh Sunday after the Epiphany)

THE WORLD

A single newspaper, a small bundle and a large bundle of papers

---

Let's suppose your class at school had a project to collect newspapers to recycle. The teacher said the papers would be sold and the money given to the class.

Some of the students brought big bundles of papers—like this *(hold up big bundle)*. Some brought small bundles—like this *(hold up small bundle)*. Some brought one newspaper—like this *(hold up single newspaper)*. Some didn't bring any—like this *(hold out empty hands)*.

When the papers were sold, the class had 10 dollars. There were 20 students in the class. If they divided the money equally, each student would get 50 cents. The children who brought no paper and those who brought only one thought the money should be divided equally. But the ones who brought the big bundles of paper thought they should get more money.

What do you think? Should each student receive 50 cents? Or should the ones who brought the most paper get the most money? According to the way we do business, it would be fair for those who did the most work to get the most money. By our system the one who works the most gets the most. The one who doesn't work, doesn't get anything. That is fair.

But God has a different way of doing things. He wants to give good to everyone, and he does not want to punish anyone. The psalm for today says, "The Lord is merciful and loving, slow to become angry and full of constant love. He does not punish us as we deserve or repay us for our sins and wrongs."

God says there is something more important than being fair: he would rather be merciful. If God were always fair with us, he would give us what we deserve. When God is merciful to us, he gives us what he wants us to have, rather than what we deserve.

Do you want God to be *fair* with you? Or do you want God to be *merciful* to you? If you think you are better than others, then you probably want to have what you think you deserve. If you brought a big bundle of paper, you would want more than the ones who brought little or nothing.

But if we ask God to be fair with us and reward us for the good we do, we are also asking him to be fair and to punish us for the bad we do. If you want what you deserve for doing good, then you also should get what you deserve for doing bad.

God does not want to give us what we deserve, because he knows about our sin. So he sent his Son Jesus to take our punishment for us. Jesus pays for our sin and gives us God's mercy. Instead of being fair with us and punishing us, he is merciful with us and forgives us.

When we see other people who do not love God or serve him as we do, remember that God loves them anyway. He gives them good things too—not because they deserve it, but because he is merciful to them, just as he is merciful to us.

Put God on the Scales

THE WORD

Trust in God at all times, my people.
Tell him all your troubles,
for he is our refuge.
Men are all like a puff of breath;
great and small alike are worthless.
Put them on the scales, and they weigh nothing;
they are lighter than a mere breath.

Psalm 62:8-9 (Eighth Sunday after the Epiphany)

THE WORLD

A balance scale, several blocks, a balloon, a cross

Do you know how to use a scale like this? *(Hold up balance scale.)* I'll show you. It is a balance scale. When both sides are empty, it is in balance. See how the sides are even with one another. When I put a block on one side, that side goes down. But if I put two blocks on the other side, that side goes down and the first side goes up. The side that has the most weight is always down.

The psalm for today tells us to use a scale to find out what we should trust in. To trust means to depend on, to have faith in. We will use the scale to decide where to put our trust.

First, on this side we will see if we can trust in the things we do. Often we trust in ourselves. We trust in how smart we are, how good-looking we are, how much money we have, or the things we can do. Each of us can do many good things, but we cannot put our trust in ourselves. The psalm says, "Men are all like a puff of breath; great and small alike are worthless. Put them on the scales, and they weigh nothing; they are lighter than a mere breath."

David, a great king, wrote these words. He was strong and brave. He became rich and famous. But he knew that all the great things he did were like a puff of breath. He did not trust in them. *(Remove blocks from scale.)*

Let me blow up this balloon to show you a puff of breath. See, there is a puff of breath. All the great things we do are like this puff of breath. When we put it on the scale, it weighs nothing. Look, the balloon does nothing to the scale.

However, David also tells us, "Trust in God at all times, my people. Tell him all your troubles, for he is our refuge." David tells us to think about the things God has done. God has created us and taken care of us. God has sent his Son Jesus to be our Savior. Jesus died for our sins and forgives us. He rose from the dead and tells us that after we die we also will come back from the grave.

The cross reminds us of the things God has done for us. *(Put cross on scale.)* The things that God has done are on one side, and the things we have done, that puff of breath, are on the other. See what happens. What God had done weighs more than what we have done. What we have done helps only ourselves; what God has done helps all people. What we have done lasts only a little while; what God has done lasts forever.

God sent Jesus to this earth so he could be on the scale with us. We do not have to depend on ourselves. We can trust in him.

From the Bottom to the Top

THE WORD

"O Zion, my sacred hill," [the Lord] says,
"I have installed my king."
"I will announce," says the king,
"what the Lord has declared.
He said to me: 'You are my son;
today I have become your father.' "

Psalm 2:6-7 (Last Sunday after the Epiphany)

THE WORLD

A tall cardboard box with an elevator made from a milk carton and a string so it may be lifted along the outside of the box

---

Pretend this box is a tall apartment building. The owners of the building want to add an elevator so people will not have to climb up the stairs. Suppose the owners installed the elevator here. *(Hold the elevator at the top of the box.)* If the elevator stayed only at the top floor, it would not help anyone. People would have to climb the stairs to get to the elevator.

On the other hand, what if the elevator were installed here? *(Put the carton at the bottom of the box.)* If the elevator stayed at the bottom, it would do no good either. People could get in it, but it wouldn't take them anywhere. The elevator must be able to go to the bottom to pick up people, then take them to the top. *(Move the carton from the bottom to the top.)*

In some ways Jesus is like this elevator. Jesus came to earth to be with us. He came down to our level. Remember Christmas, when we talked about the birth of Jesus? He was born down here *(put the carton at the bottom)*

42

with us. We can come to Jesus, because he came to be with us.

Today we think about the transfiguration, when three disciples saw Jesus at the top. They saw him in heaven with Moses and Elijah. Jesus belongs there too. The psalm quotes God when he said, "On Zion, my sacred hill, I have installed my king." Then the king tells us who he is. He says, " I will announce what the Lord has declared. He said to me: 'You are my son; today I have become your father.' " The king is Jesus, God's Son who came to earth. He has been installed on Zion, the sacred hill. He is ruler of heaven, at the top. *(Hold the carton at the top.)*

For the elevator to do its job, it must be able to move from the bottom to the top. It cannot be only in one place or the other. In the same way Jesus moves from the bottom to the top so he can be our Savior. Long ago he came to the bottom to live with people. He was tempted to sin; he felt pain and sorrow, he even died to pay for our sins. Yet Jesus remains with us. He has promised to be a part of our lives. He is like an elevator that comes down to the ground floor to pick us up where we are.

Jesus did not stay on the ground floor. He rose from the dead. He came to lift us up to be with God who created us and loves us. Jesus is the king on Zion's hill. He is the Son of God who rules in heaven. But he is not alone there. He came to earth to save us so we can be in heaven with him.

At times we need to see Jesus at the bottom with us. At other times we need to see him in his glory so we know where he is taking us. He came to be with us at the bottom so we can be with him at the top.

If God Kept Records

THE WORD

Hear my cry, O Lord;
Listen to my call for help!
If you kept a record of our sins,
who would escape being condemned?
But you forgive us,
so that we should reverently obey you.

Psalm 130:2-4 (First Sunday in Lent)

THE WORLD

Five file folders with names of children on the tabs and one with the name Jesus Christ, a pad of paper and pencil

---

The psalm for today asks an important question: if God kept a record of our sins, who would escape being condemned?

Let's imagine the kind of record of sin God might keep. He could have files like these. See, each file has the name of a person on it. God could write a note to himself each time we sinned and file it under our names. Brad lied to his mother on Wednesday. *(Write:* LIE *and the date. Put the paper in Brad's file.)* Susan stole a bag of potato chips from the store. *(Record it and file.)* Mark used God's name in a bad way by cursing someone. *(Record it.)*

Think about the sins God would have recorded in your file if he kept records like this. He would have a piece of paper for each wrong thing you have done. He also would have a piece of paper to show the things we did not do that we should have done. If God kept such a record of sins, my file would be very big. I am sure yours would be too.

44

However, the psalm does *not* tell us that God keeps a record of our sins. Instead, the psalm writer thanks God for *not* keeping such a record. He says, "If you kept a record of our sins, who would escape being condemned? But you forgive us." Instead of keeping a record of our sins, God forgives the sins. He does not want to keep the sins in a file. He wants to throw them away.

Jesus came to earth to wipe out the record of our sins. He is our brother, so he also has a file. See, here is the file with his name. He was tempted to sin in every way that we are tempted, but he did not sin. See, his file is empty. Yet he is the one who was punished for sin. Because he loved us, he asked that all of our sins be put in his file. The lying, the stealing, the cursing, all the other things we have done wrong, were put in the file with his name on it. *(Move all the papers to file marked JESUS.)* Our files are now empty. God has no record of our sins.

The one who wrote this psalm felt free to ask God for help, because he knew his sins were forgiven. He said, "Hear my cry, O Lord; listen to my call for help!" He was not afraid to talk to God. He did not worry that God would look in his file, see his sin, and then refuse to listen to his prayer. You can also ask God for help. God has no record of your sin.

Because God has forgiven our sins, we do not have to give up in our fight against sin. When God forgives us, he also helps us stop sinning. The psalm says, "But you forgive us, so that we should reverently obey you." We can obey God, not because we are afraid he will keep a list of our sin, but because he has forgiven us. Each day we can start out with an empty file. Our past sins don't have to pull us back into more sin. Jesus has made us free.

Go to the Lord for Help

THE WORD

Go to the Lord for help;
and worship him continually.
The Lord is our God;
his commands are for all the world.
He will keep his covenant forever,
his promises for a thousand generations.

Psalm 105:4, 7-8 (Second Sunday in Lent

THE WORLD

A red balloon with a sad face and a blue balloon with a
happy face, each filled with helium or on a long stick

A teacher took her class of 27 second-graders to a zoo.
Maybe you don't know it yet, but it is difficult to keep 27
second-graders together. That day many other children
were also visiting the zoo.

This teacher had a clever way to call all 27 students
together at the same time. If she missed a child or if someone misbehaved, she would put up this balloon *(hold up
red one)*. The children could see the sad face. They knew
that it meant something was wrong. They would all come
back to the teacher.

The teacher also had another balloon. When she found
something that all the children would enjoy—like the
monkey show or a clown—she would put up the other
balloon *(hold up blue one)*. Then the students would
know that something good was going to happen. They
would all come back to the teacher.

Other people at the zoo could tell which children were
in this teacher's class. Her students would always go to
her when she put up either of the balloons.

46

The psalm for today shows us that God is like that teacher. We are like the students. It says, "Go to the Lord for help; and worship him continually. We need to go to God when we need help, and we need to go to God to worship him when we are happy. In this world we all need God, just as the second-graders needed their teacher at the zoo.

God also has a special way to call us to himself. The psalm says, "The Lord is our God; his commands are for all the world." God has given commandments to all people. He wants to protect us; so he tells us things we should do and things we should not do. His commandments are like this balloon *(hold up red one)*. When we hear the commandments, we know we need to go to God for his help.

God also has another balloon. The psalm says, "[God] will keep his covenant forever, his promises for a thousand generations." God promises to be with us all the time. Long ago he promised to send a Savior. He kept that promise when Jesus came to die for our sins and to give us a new life. Jesus promises to hear our prayers, to love us, and to take us to heaven. His promises are like this balloon *(hold up blue one)*. When we see the promises, we come to God to worship him.

When you hear God's message in the Bible, you see his two balloons. You hear his commands, and you hear his promises. Both of them invite you to come to God for help. When you go to God, the people in the world know you belong to him. Then they can see that the messages are for them too.

Take Your Complaints to God

THE WORD

I call to the Lord for help;
I plead with him.
I bring him all my complaints;
I tell him all my troubles.
When I am ready to give up,
he knows what I should do.

Psalm 142:1-3a (Third Sunday in Lent)

THE WORLD

A sack containing a library book, a letter, and a box
marked COMPLAINTS

Here is a bag of things I want you to deliver for me
(hold up sack). You have to decide where to take each
of the things in the sack. First, here is a book. Where
would you take it? See this card inside the cover? You
would take the book to the library. Where would you take
this *(hold up the letter)?* It is stamped and addressed;
that means it is ready to be mailed. So you would take it
to the post office.

What about this *(show them the box)?* Where would
you take it? The box is labeled COMPLAINTS. Pretend that
the box is filled with all the things you gripe about. Help
me name the things in the box. What do you complain
about? What are your troubles? *(Help the children identify complaints about rules at home regarding bedtime,
food, watching TV, etc. Search for other complaints about
school, friends, etc.)* Now we have all of our complaints
in this box. What are we going to do with them? We took
the book back to the library and the letter to the post office. Where do we take the complaints?

In Psalm 142 David tells us what to do with our complaints. He says, "I call to the Lord for help; I plead with him. I bring him all my complaints; I tell him all my troubles. When I am ready to give up, he knows what I should do."

David wrote this psalm while he was hiding in a cave. He had lots of troubles. He could complain about many things. His enemies were trying to kill him. He thought all his family and friends had forgotten him. He had to stay in the cave; yet he knew he could take his troubles to God. David knew he did not have to go to the temple to pray to God. God could hear from his hiding place in the cave. David told God all his problems. He complained about everything that bothered him. He felt like giving up, but when he asked God for help, God told him what to do. David got rid of all his complaints, because he gave them to God.

You and I can also take our complaints to God. God sent Jesus to live on this earth to receive our complaints. We go to Jesus to tell him about our troubles; we confess our sins to him; we ask him for help. Jesus gives us the help we need. He died to pay for our sins. He rose from the dead to live with us so he can help and protect us.

After you go past the library, you don't have the book anymore, because you returned it. You don't have the letter any more, because you mailed it. You also get rid of your complaints when you take them to God. You give them to him, and he takes care of them for you. The next time you hear yourself complaining, put all of your gripes in a box. Take them to God. He'll get rid of them for you.

Let God Defend You

O God, declare me innocent,
and defend my cause against the ungodly;
deliver me from lying and evil men!
Psalm 43:1 (Fourth Sunday in Lent)

THE WORLD

A glass-covered picture, black grease pencil, and paper napkin

---

Pretend this is a picture of you. It's a good picture. It shows how neat, bright-eyed, and nice you are. God created you to be a good person. You are a good person, but you are also something else. Something has been added to your picture. *(Draw a mustache on the picture with the grease pencil.)* Now it is not a good picture because something has been added to ruin it. Sin has also been added to your life. Sin ruins the beauty of God's creation. Because of sin, we have a hard time seeing the good that God created in us.

All of us have sin in our lives. What can we do about it? Some try to hide the sin. *(Try to hold the picture with your hand over the mustache.)* But when we hide the sin in us, we also hide the good that God has created in us. That does not work.

Some people try to show off their sin as though it were a good thing. That's like trying to say the mustache makes the picture better. They become proud of their faults. But the truth is that the mustache ruins the picture. Sin also ruins our lives.

There is another way to get help when we sin. You can let God help you. The person who wrote our psalm for

50

today shows us this other way. He remembered that God had created him to be good; therefore he knew God wanted him to be good. So when he did wrong, he went back to God and asked for help. He said, "O God, declare me innocent, and defend my cause against the ungodly; deliver me from lying and evil men!"

The psalmist knows he cannot defend himself. He can't hide his sin. He knows that others will lie about him and make his sin sound even worse than it is. So he asks God to help him. He wants God to defend him. If we had never done anything wrong, it would be easy for God to defend us. But even when we have done wrong things, we can ask God to defend us.

God is willing to help us. He will declare us innocent, even though we have done wrong. That does not mean we have fooled God by hiding our sin from him. It does not mean that he pretends we have not sinned. Instead, the God who created us to be good has made us good again.

God did this by sending Jesus to be our Savior. Jesus is like this napkin. He comes to us and wipes our sin away. *(Wipe the grease off the glass.)* Now the picture is clean again. The marks are all gone. Jesus took our sin away.

Do you know where the sin went? Look, it is on the napkin. *(Show them.)* Jesus took the sin off of us and put it on himself. That's why he had to die for us. I can now keep this picture, because it is clean. But I will throw the napkin away, because it is dirty. Jesus was punished for us, so we would not have to be punished.

When Jesus died on the cross, he took our sin away. Three days later he came back. Now, because he has taken away our sin, we can be with him.

Don't Be Afraid of Death

THE WORD

The danger of death was all around me;
the horrors of the grave closed in on me;
I was filled with fear and anxiety.
Then I called to the Lord,
"I beg you, Lord, save me!"

Psalm 116:3-4 (Fifth Sunday in Lent)

THE WORLD

A grocery sack containing a soft drink in a plastic bottle

Meagan's class at school was going on a field trip to visit a fire house. The teacher asked Meagan to carry this sack. It has a big bottle of soft drink in it. Meagan knew she and all the other students would enjoy a drink on the field trip. She carried the bottle very carefully. She did not want to drop it and break the bottle.

Several times she almost let the sack slip out of her hand. Each time the other children told her to be more careful. "Don't let the bottle break," they said, "because we are thirsty." Then just as Meagan was going up a ladder *(hold the sack high)*, the sack slipped from her hand and fell *(drop it)*.

Meagan was sure the bottle had broken. She hurried down the ladder and picked up the sack. Look, the drink was not in a glass bottle. It was in a plastic bottle. A glass bottle would have broken, but the plastic bottle did not break. All through the trip Meagan had worried that she might drop the bottle and it would break. But she need not have worried. Even when she dropped the sack, the bottle did not break.

The psalm for today is about someone who also worried. He was not worried about breaking something. He was worried about dying. Listen to what he said, "The danger of death was all around me; the horrors of the grave closed in on me; I was filled with fear and anxiety."

Maybe the man was sick and afraid he would die. Maybe he was a soldier going to fight and knew that many soldiers get killed. Maybe one of his friends or someone in his family had died. He knew that some day he would die too. He was afraid.

A person who is afraid to die worries. Such a person is like Meagan when she was afraid she would drop the bottle and it would break. People who worry about dying think death will destroy them. If they worry about dying, they cannot enjoy living.

The person who wrote the psalm worried for a long time. But he found an answer for his worry. He said, "Then I called to the Lord, 'I beg you, Lord save me!'" He knew he couldn't save his own life. He also knew he would have to die sometime. So he asked God for help.

You and I do not have to worry about dying. We can use the same prayer the psalm writer used. We can say, "I beg you, Lord, save me!" God answered that prayer—and our prayer—when he sent Jesus to die in our place. When Jesus died, he did it to pay for our sins. If we had to die to pay for our own sins, then death would destroy us. But Jesus took away our sin, so death will not destroy us.

We are like this plastic bottle. The bottle will not break when it is dropped. When Meagan thought it would break, she worried about dropping it. If we worry that death will destroy us, then we have to worry about dying. But when we know Christ freed us from the punishment of death, we do not have to be afraid any more. We will die—just as Meagan dropped the bottle. But the bottle didn't break. And death won't destroy us.

Where Will You Go for Help?

THE WORD

I come to you, Lord for protection;
never let me be defeated.
You are a righteous God;
save me, I pray!
  Psalm 31:1 (The Sunday of the Passion—Palm Sunday)

THE WORLD

Figure of a child about six inches tall (use a doll, or cut a figure from cardboard), a coffee cup, a pencil, and a book

---

Suppose this figure is you *(show figure of child)*. You are playing a game, and you need to find a place to hide. Let me help you look for a place to go so your friends can't find you.

There's a tub *(show the cup)*. You could try to hide in it. *(Put the doll in the cup.)* But the tub is too short, or you are too tall. So you can't hide in it. There's a pole *(show pencil)*. It is taller than you are, so you can hide behind it. *(Put the figure behind the pencil.)* The pole is tall enough to hide you, but it is not wide enough, or you are not thin enough. So you can't hide behind the pole.

There's a wall *(show book)*. The wall is taller than you and it is wider than you. You can hide behind the wall. *(Place the figure behind the book.)* Now no one can see you.

Now let's talk about something that is not a game. You have done and said things that are wrong. We call these wrong things *sin*. We also sin when we do not do and say the things we should do and say. You need help.

In the game you need a place to hide. In real life you need a place to get rid of your sin. Where will you go for help?

Other people cannot get rid of your sin for you. All of the rest of us are sinners too. If you try to hide your sins behind me, you would be like the doll hiding in the tub. I cannot hide your sins. No one else can either. We are all sinners. We can't hide our own sins.

The person who wrote today's psalm found someone to help him. He said, "I come to you, Lord, for protection; never let me be defeated. You are a righteous God; save me, I pray!"

The psalmist knew that if he wanted to get rid of his sin he had to find someone who was righteous—that is, someone who is holy and without sin. We can't hide sin behind sin. We need to find good to cover evil.

So the psalmist asked God for help. He said, "You are a righteous God; save me, I pray!" And God heard his prayer. He sent Jesus to be the one who would get rid of our sin. Jesus was holy, without sin. Yet he died for us to pay for our sin. His goodness covers our evil. When we are with Jesus, no one can see our sin. It is not just hidden; it is forgiven.

I want you to know about Jesus so you can always go to him for help. Long ago children in Jerusalem saw Jesus and said, "Hosanna! Hosanna!" That meant "Save me, I pray," the same thing that the psalmist said. Those children showed their love for Jesus by praising him and asking him for help. We also praise Jesus by coming to him and receiving the forgiveness he earned for us by his suffering and death. He is the one to ask for help, because he is the one who can give us help.

I Will Not Die

THE WORD

I will not die; instead, I will live
and proclaim what the Lord has done.
He has punished me severely,
but he has not let me die.

Psalm 118:17-18 (Easter Sunday)

THE WORLD

A plastic glass and a cut-glass tumbler

You might see either of these glasses on a dinner table. This one is made of plastic. Your mother might use it for a picnic or for a family meal when she is busy and doesn't have time to wash dishes. This one is valuable cut glass. It is old. Your mother would use it only on special occasions.

Suppose your mother broke the plastic glass. *(Crack it.)* What would she do? She would throw it away and use another one just like it. But what if she chipped a piece out of this one *(show the cut-glass one)*? Would she throw it away? Of course not. She would keep the pieces and have someone glue it back together. A skilled person could repair this glass so no one could see the crack.

Think of God as being the mother in the story I told. Think of yourself as being one of the glasses. Which glass are you like? What happens if you are broken, if you do something wrong, if you fail to do what you should do? Does God throw you away as your mother would throw away the plastic glass? Or does God repair you, as your mother would have had this glass repaired?

The one who wrote the psalm for today knew what God would do. He said, "I will not die; instead, I will live and proclaim what the Lord has done. He has punished me severely, but he has not let me die." The psalm writer knew himself, and he knew God. He knew he had done wrong. He knew he would be punished. But he knew God would not throw him away. God would repair him. God would forgive him and give him a new life.

You and I can also know God, and we can know what God will do. We can see what he did when he sent Jesus to be our Savior. Jesus suffered and died for us. He was like a glass that was broken. He was buried. It looked as though God treated him like the plastic glass thrown away. But three days later Jesus came back from the dead. He had been broken by death, but he had been made whole and alive again. Jesus destroyed the power of death. He showed the world that death does not have to destroy us. Even as he died, he would say, "I will not die; instead, I will live and proclaim what the Lord has done." He knew he could come back to life again.

Because Jesus lives, you will live also. God will not throw you away because you have sinned. Even when you die, you can say, "I will not die, instead, I will live and proclaim what the Lord has done." The Lord has died for you. He has come back from the grave for you. When you die, he will also bring you back from the grave.

Today we rejoice that Jesus is alive. We proclaim what he has done. We know we will always live with him.

Don't Forget the Greatest

THE WORD

Give thanks to the Lord, proclaim his greatness;
tell the nations what he has done.
Sing praise to the Lord;
tell the wonderful things he has done.
                    Psalm 105:1-2 (Second Sunday of Easter)

THE WORLD

A watch (or other family heirloom) wrapped as a gift
with a bell or other trinket tied to the bow, and a thank-
you letter

A man gave this gift to his grandson *(show the gift)*.
See how pretty it is. Look, it even has a little bell on the
bow. Listen to the bell when I shake it.

But the important part of the gift is not what is on the
outside. The important gift is on the inside. I'll open it.
Look, here is a watch. It is special because the man had
received it from his grandfather. Now the man is giving
it to his grandson. That is a special gift that the boy will
keep all of his life and maybe give to his grandson.

Suppose the boy wrote this thank-you letter to his
grandfather: "Dear Grandpa. Thank you for the gift. I
liked the little bell very much. I put it on a ribbon around
my cat's neck. You should see her when she runs and
plays. She and I like the bell very much. Thanks again.
Your grandson."

Something is wrong with that letter. It thanks the grandfather for the little gift and doesn't say anything about
the big gift. The bell was a nice little extra decoration,
but it may soon be lost. The boy will keep the watch all
of his life.

Maybe we make the same mistake that boy made when we thank God. Listen to our Bible reading for today because it tells us how to give thanks to God. "Give thanks to the Lord, proclaim his greatness; tell the nations what he has done. Sing praise to the Lord; tell the wonderful things he has done."

Notice that the psalm says we thank God by telling others about the greatness of God. We talk about the wonderful things God has done. When the grandfather wrapped his gift to the boy and put the bell on it, the bell was a nice little extra gift. But the bell was not the important gift. It did not show the wonderful thing the man was doing for his grandson.

God gives us many little gifts too. I hope you thank him when you get good grades, win ball games, and take special trips. Thank him for meals, your home, your clothing, and many other good things. But don't forget the greatness of God. Remember the most wonderful thing he has done.

The greatest gift God has given you is Jesus Christ. Christ has lived on this earth. He died to take away your sin. He rose from the dead to give you a life that will never end. He lives with you today. Even though you have not seen him, Jesus is with you. He loves you, forgives you, and gives you many blessings.

Remember how to thank God. Tell everyone about the great gift he has given to all people. Remember the other gifts too—but don't forget the greatest of all.

God Will Never Throw You Away

THE WORD

And so I am thankful and glad,
and I feel completely secure,
because you protect me from the power of death,
and the one you love you will not abandon to the world
of the dead.

Psalm 16:9-10 (Third Sunday of Easter)

THE WORLD

The children and the things they have with them

I want each of you to think of the things you have with you right now. Think about the clothes you are wearing. Some of you are wearing glasses. Do any of you have braces on your teeth? Do you have a ring, a necklace, money?

How long do you think you will keep the things you have now? If you have money, it will probably be gone soon. A year from now you will have worn out or outgrown the clothes you have now. You will either give them away or throw them away. If you wear glasses, you will need new ones in a year or so. You'll get rid of the braces on your teeth. If you have a ring or other jewelry, you might keep it even after you can no longer wear it.

As you go through life, you will always get new things and throw old things away. You will keep some things for only a short time. You will keep some things a long time. If I see you ten years from now, you probably will not have anything with you that you have now.

However, you will still be you. You will still have your name. You will still have your body, mind, and soul. You will look different, but you will be you. Everything you own will some day be thrown away or given away. But what about you? At the end of your life what will happen to you? Will you also be thrown away?

The psalm for today answers that question with a *no*. It says, "And so I am thankful and glad, and I feel completely secure, because you protect me from the power of death, and the one you love you will not abandon to the world of the dead."

You don't have to worry that God will ever throw you away. You will not wear out. He will not lose you or forget you. He will not leave you behind. He will not find someone else to love and trade you in, because he already loves all people. Even when the time comes for you to die, God will still be with you. He will not leave you in the place of the dead. You will not stay in a grave. Instead he will bring you back to life again so you may live with him forever in heaven.

Jesus died and was buried. Three days later he rose from the dead. Because he won a victory over death, he can give you a victory too. Jesus keeps God's promise not to abandon you to the world of the dead.

When we see each other in heaven, we will not have the same clothes, glasses, rings, and other things that we have now. But we will be with each other and with Jesus. God will never throw you away.

I Have Everything I Need

THE WORD

The Lord is my shepherd; I have everything I need.
He lets me rest in fields of green grass
and leads me to quiet pools of fresh water.
He gives me new strength.
He guides me in the right paths, as he has promised.

Psalm 23:1-3 (Fourth Sunday of Easter)

THE WORLD

A first-aid kit, a collection of individual items included in the kit, and a box

---

Is your family ready in case someone has an accident? Little accidents often happen at home or when a family is on a trip. The hurt is not bad enough to go to the hospital, but it still needs treatment. So we need medical supplies at home. We call these things first aid.

Suppose your family decided to have first-aid supplies ready at home in case they were needed. You would have to go to the store to buy what you need. You would buy tape *(name each item you have collected and show them)*, gauze, bandages of different sizes, something to clean the wounds, something to relieve pain, etc. You would also need a box to keep all of these things in so you could find them when you need them.

As you go through the store to buy all of these things, you might see this *(hold up first-aid kit)*. This kit has all the things you need for an emergency. They are neatly packed into one handy box you can keep at home and take along in the car on trips. Instead of buying many things and a box to store them in, you can buy the first-aid kit and have all you need in one place.

We have talked about first aid for injuries to your body. We also have injuries to our soul. We also need help in our spiritual injuries. When we sin, we need forgiveness. When we are afraid, we need faith. When we are lonely, we need love. When we don't know what to do, we need wisdom. When we die, we need a victory over death. Where would you look for all of those things?

Our Bible reading for today is Psalm 23. It says: "The Lord is my shepherd; I have everything I need. He lets me rest in fields of green grass and leads me to quiet pools of fresh water. He gives me new strength. He guides me in the right paths, as he has promised."

Jesus is the shepherd who came from God to take care of us. When he is with us, we have everything we need. He is like the first-aid kit. He died for us to pay for our sins. He is with us at all times, so we do not have to be afraid or lonely. He guides us, so we know how to live. He rose from the dead to give us a new life that will never end.

We do not have to look in many different places to find our spiritual first aid. We do not have to collect our own ways to solve our problems. Jesus is the good shepherd who gives us everything we need. He is with us all the time—in our home, at school, on trips. He always gives his help.

God Does What He Says

THE WORD

The words of the Lord are true,
and all his works are dependable.
The Lord loves what is righteous and just;
his constant love fills the earth.

Psalm 33:4-5 (Fifth Sunday of Easter)

THE WORLD

Five blocks

I am going to teach something that some of you already know. If you already know, I want you to think how you learned what I am teaching.

First I will tell you: two plus three equals five. If you already know how to add numbers, you know what I said is true: two plus three equals five. If you did not know, you know now. You know that two plus three equals five.

New let me teach you the same thing another way. *(Show two blocks. Point to each one and place them on one hand. Now point to each of the other three. Place them in the other hand. Hold your two hands together so the five blocks are in a row.)*

First I *told* you two plus three equals five. Then I *showed* you two plus three equals five. You can learn by *hearing* and you can learn by *seeing.*

The psalm for today tells us that God also teaches us by what he says and by what he does. It says, "The words of the Lord are true, and all his works are dependable. The Lord loves what is righteous and just; his constant love fills the earth."

God wants you to know he is righteous and just. That

64

means he is fair and good. He wants you to know he loves the whole world. He says his love fills the earth.

God teaches us about himself in two ways. First he tells us, just as I told you two plus three equals five. God *says* he loves us. The psalm says, "The words of the Lord are true." We can believe God when he says he loves us. We learn by *hearing what he says.*

We can also learn about God by *seeing what he does.* The psalm says, "All his works are dependable." God *tells* us the truth, and he *shows* us the truth. We can learn about his love by seeing what he does.

You can see God loves you by the way he created you. He gave you a body, mind, and soul. He placed you in a beautiful world he created. You can see God loves you because he sent his Son Jesus to be your Savior. Jesus *tells* you he loves you. He also *shows* you he loves you by what he did for you. He suffered and died to pay for your sin. He rose from the dead to give you a life that will never end.

When we read the Bible, we still *hear* God tell us that he loves us. We also *see* God's love for us when we see what he does for us today. When you were baptized in the name of the Father, Son, and the Holy Spirit, God not only said he loved you but he also showed his love for you. When you see how God works through people who help you, who teach you, who take care of you, you are seeing how God loves you. When God hears your prayers, when he forgives you, you know he loves you.

God does what he says. He *says* he loves you. He *shows* he loves you.

Who Makes the First Move?

THE WORD
Come and see what God has done,
his wonderful acts among men.
I will bring burnt offerings to your house;
I will offer you what I promised.
                    Psalm 66:5, 13 (Sixth Sunday of Easter)

THE WORLD
A locked case (briefcase, jewelry box, or small suitcase), the key, and enough peanuts for each child to have a handful

---

I want you to do something for me. Will you? Okay, I want you to give a peanut to someone. Would you please do that? Of course, you can't give someone else a peanut if you don't have a peanut. I've asked *you* to do something. I will give you some peanuts. I'll give you a handful so you can have some for yourself and some to give away, as I asked you to do.

This case has lots of peanuts in it. Help yourself. Oh yes, the case is locked. I have the key. Before you can take the peanuts, I must open the case. I'll unlock it. Now help yourself to some peanuts. (*Let children do that.*) Remember I want you to have some for yourself—and some to give to your mother or father or someone else.

Before you go to share your peanuts, I want you to think about what we just did. I asked you to do something, but you couldn't do it. I had to do something first. I had to make the first move. Before you could give peanuts away, I had to give you peanuts. Before you could take the peanuts, I had to unlock the case.

God also asks us to do things. He asks us to obey his

commands. He asks us to love one another. He asks us to believe in Jesus Christ. Before we can do what he asks us to do, God has to do something. He has to make the first move. God made the first move when he sent Jesus to live with us. Jesus died to pay for sin and rose from the dead so we can believe in him. Jesus obeyed God's commands for us. First God loved *us,* so we can love *him.*

God has made the first move. He loves us. You have the peanuts I gave to you. Soon you can do what I first asked you to do. You can give some of them to someone else. Of course, you could keep them all for yourself, but I hope you will share them.

You could also keep all the good things God has given you for yourself, but I hope you do not. The psalm for today tells you to remember the great things God has done for you. It says, "Come and see what God has done, his wonderful acts among men." Every time we talk about Jesus, we see the great things God has done for us. I often tell you about Jesus so you will know how much God loves you and what he has given you.

The psalm also says, "I will bring burnt offerings to your house; I will offer you what I promised." When the psalms were written, the people showed their love for God by giving burnt offerings as sacrifices. Jesus has asked us to show our love for him by loving one another.

Remember, God has made the first move. He has loved you. He has given you many ways to love others. Because God has saved you, you can now serve him. You can make the next move. *(Encourage the children to go and share the peanuts with others in the congregation.)*

Who Leads the Leader?

THE WORD

Clap your hands for joy, all peoples!
Praise God with loud songs!
The Lord, the Most High, is to be feared;
he is a great king, ruling over all the world.
He gave us victory over the peoples;
he made us rule over the nations.

Psalm 47:1-3 (Seventh Sunday of Easter)

THE WORLD

A rope about five or six feet long

Sometimes each one of us will be a leader, and sometimes we will be followers. Let me show you the difference with this rope. *(Hand one end of the rope to a child.)* You hold one end of the rope; I'll hold the other. If I pull you, I am the leader and you are the follower. If you pull me, you are the leader and I am the follower. When we have a children's sermon like this, I am the leader. I teach you about Jesus. You are the follower, and you learn about the Savior. If I came to your house and you showed me your room, you would be the leader. I would follow you because you know the way to your room.

The psalm for today says God is our leader. "The Lord, the Most High, is to be feared; he is a great king, ruling over all the world." To fear God is to respect him, not to be afraid of him. God is the Most High, the great king who rules all the world. He leads us. *(Hold the rope in the middle.)* He is the leader, and you are the follower.

When you learn about Jesus, you see how God leads you. Jesus came to live with us to lead us to God. He leads us away from temptation and sin. He leads us to

God's love and grace. Jesus leads us to people who will help us—and to people we can help. When we die, he will lead us through death to eternal life.

You can see why the psalm says, "Clap your hands for joy, all peoples! Praise God with loud songs!" We are happy that God is our leader. The psalm also says, "He gave us victory over the peoples; he made us rule over the nations." God is our leader, and we are his followers. But sometimes he asks us to be leaders so others can follow us. Sometimes he asks others to be leaders for us to follow.

(Hand one end of rope to same child.) Hold on to one end of the rope again. You are the follower now. God holds this end of the rope. He is the leader. God has other followers who are your leaders. Think of your parents, teachers, and others. Pretend they are holding the middle of the rope. God, who has this end, is leading them. When they follow God, they are leading you so you can follow God too.

Sometimes you are a leader. When you take care of a little brother or sister or when you have a special job at school, you are a leader. Then you hold the rope in the middle. God leads you; you lead those who follow you.

All of your leaders on earth need a leader. That is God. When you are a leader, you also need a leader. God is the Most High, the leader of us all.

Don't Lose Your Breath

THE WORD
> But when you [God] give them breath, they are created;
> you give new life to the earth.
>
> Psalm 104:30 (The Day of Pentecost)

THE WORLD
A balloon

When God created the first man Adam, he made his body first. The body was like this balloon. It seemed empty. Then God breathed life-giving breath into his nose, and Adam began to live. God not only gave the man a body, he also made the body alive, like this *(blow up the balloon)*. Now the balloon seems real. I can squeeze it, and it pushes back. I can feel the air inside.

God has also given you his breath. Breathe in and feel your breath as you blow the air out. We have to breathe to live. No one taught you how to breathe. You do it all the time without even thinking about it. When you do think about your breath, you can remember how God created you.

The word *breath* in the Bible means the air you breathe in and out. It also means your soul or spirit. When God gave you breath, he not only gave you air, but he gave you life itself. Adam's life came from God; so his life was like God's. God's life will never end, and he gave us a life that will not end.

When I let some of the air out of the balloon, it becomes soft and flabby. *(Demonstrate.)* The balloon seems to lose its life. When you sin, you turn away from God. You lose the closeness to God. When you do wrong, you are no longer as God made you to be. You lose part of your life with God.

The psalm for today speaks to you when you are losing your breath, when you are turning away from God. The one who wrote the psalm is talking to God, and he says, "But when you give them breath, they are created; you give new life to the earth." God not only gave you the breath of life when you were born, but he continues to give you breath. He gave you life; he also gives you new life.

Jesus came to earth to give you that new life. He was like this balloon. *(Blow it up.)* He was full of life, but our sins caused him to lose his life. He died for us. *(Let the air out.)* But three days later he came back to life. *(Blow up the balloon again.)* He had life; he lost it; he had new life again.

Jesus promised that the Holy Spirit would come and give us new life too. The Holy Spirit is God's life-giver. When we were created, we received our spirit, our breath of life. As long as we live on earth, we will always be losing our life. *(Let some air from the balloon.)* We cannot depend on ourselves to keep our life. *(Let out more air.)* But the Holy Spirit comes to us again and again. When we hear the story of Jesus and his love for us, he gives us new life. *(Blow more air into the balloon.)* He gives us new life when he gives us forgiveness. *(Add more air.)*

Even when we stop breathing and die, our life will not be destroyed. God gave us our spirit. He will also keep our spirit.

Listen for the Right Voice

Praise the Lord you heavenly beings;
praise his glory and power.
Praise the Lord's glorious name;
bow down before the Holy One when he appears. . . .
The voice of the Lord is heard
in all its might and majesty.

Psalm 29:1-2, 4 (First Sunday after Pentecost)

THE WORLD

A cassette player with a tape of Psalm 29 and a radio

Please listen to Psalm 29. It is on this tape. *(Turn on the tape player and the radio at the same time, both the same volume. After a short time turn both off.)*

Could you hear what the psalm said? It was hard to hear, because the radio was playing too. The two sounds blocked each other out. You couldn't understand either of them.

God wants to speak to us. He has important things to tell us. Sometimes we can't hear him, because we are listening to many other sounds at the same time. Think of all the voices you hear: friends, television, parents, teachers, baby sitters, brothers and sisters, radio and more. Each of those sounds can be good. God could even speak to you through each of them. But often there are too many sounds. We hear a lot and understand nothing. The voice of God gets lost in the sounds of the world.

However, there is a way to hear God. Listen to this tape without the radio. *(Rewind the tape and play the first two verses.)* The psalmist says we are to praise God. But that's part of the problem. How can we praise God if we can't hear him? When we hear so many voices, we can't hear God, so we have no reason to praise him. But the psalm tells us how God gets our attention. It says, "Bow down before the Holy One when he appears."

When something important happens, we listen. If you are talking on the phone or listening to TV while your parents are talking, you can't hear them. But if they talk about something you want to hear, such as a family trip, you'll listen. You'll hang up the phone. You'll turn off TV. You'll say "Hush!" to your brothers and sisters. And you'll listen.

When the Holy One—that's God—appears, we say "Hush!" to the world. When Jesus speaks, we turn off the other sounds; we stop our own voices; we listen. Then we hear Jesus say, "Ask, and you will receive; seek, and you will find; knock, and the door will be opened to you" (Matt. 7:7). He says, "Whoever believes and is baptized will be saved" (Mark 16:16). He says, "There are many rooms in my Father's house, and I am going to prepare a place for you" (John 14:2). He says, "I will be with you always" (Matt. 28:20).

The psalm says, "The voice of the Lord is heard in all its might and majesty." That voice is still heard today when we hear what Jesus says to us. Listen for the right voice.

When Do You Need Protection?

THE WORD

I come to you, Lord, for protection;
never let me be defeated.
You are a righteous God;
save me, I pray! . . .
You are my refuge and defense;
guide me and lead me as you have promised.
>   Psalm 31:1, 3 (Second Sunday after Pentecost)

THE WORLD

A sack containing a straw hat, a long-sleeved shirt and sun lotion

---

Dan was happy because his friend's family had invited him to go on an all-day fishing trip. He liked to be with his friend, and he liked to fish. Dan was even willing to get up early in the morning on the big day. His mother gave him this sack. It contains a hat, a shirt, and lotion. She told him these were to protect him from the sun.

Dan did not like his mother to tell him what to do. He took the sack, but when he walked outside, he felt the cool air. He thought he didn't need to be protected from the sun, so he left the sack in the carport.

When Dan and his friend were fishing, the sun was very hot. His face and arms turned red. He wished he had the hat and shirt to protect him from the sun. He thought how nice the lotion would feel. Finally, Dan had to quit fishing—just when everyone else was catching the big ones. The next day Dan was sick, because the sun had overheated him.

When Dan's mother told him he needed protection from the sun, Dan didn't think he needed the help. Later he realized he did need protection. But he had left the sack in the carport.

I told you the story about Dan to help you understand that you need Jesus to protect you. Jesus protected you from sin when he died on the cross for you. He protected you from the grave by rising from the dead and telling you that you will rise from the dead too.

Some people don't think they need Jesus. They want to take care of themselves. Later they will learn they do need him. They need Jesus' love and forgiveness. They need his power and help. But if they do not learn the story about Jesus, if they leave him behind, they will not know that Jesus wants to help them. They will think they are alone in their troubles.

When David wrote Psalm 31, he was in trouble. He knew he needed help. He also knew God loved him and would help him. He said, "I come to you, Lord, for protection; never let me be defeated. You are a righteous God; save me, I pray! . . . You are my refuge and defense; guide me and lead me as you have promised."

When David was a little boy, his mother and father told him about God. He did not reject what they told him. He knew God promised to be with him. So when he needed help, he could ask God for help. If Dan had taken along the sack that his mother gave him, he could have had protection from the sun. David took his faith with him, so he had help available.

That's why I want to tell you about Jesus today. You may not have any big problems today. You may think you don't need protection. But some day you will. If you listen to the message of Jesus's love for you now, you will know where to go for help later when you need his protection.

When Do You Need God?

THE WORD

The Almighty God, the Lord, speaks:
"Let the giving of thanks be your sacrifice to God,
and give the Almighty all that you promised.
Call to me when trouble comes;
I will save you, and you will praise me."
Psalm 50:1a, 14-15 (Third Sunday after Pentecost)

THE WORLD

A pitcher and four glasses. Fill two glasses and the pitcher with a fruit drink

Let's pretend this pitcher is God and we are the glasses. The pitcher is filled with a good drink. That reminds us God is filled with love, mercy, forgiveness, grace, and other gifts he wants to pour into our lives.

Now look at the glasses. Two are empty. Two are filled with the same drink that is in the pitcher. Which ones need the pitcher? That's easy: the empty ones. So we fill them also. *(Demonstrate.)*

Now think about ourselves and others. Who needs God? That's easy. People who are hungry, sick, guilty, lonely, afraid—they need God. In the psalm for today, God says, "Call to me when trouble comes; I will save you." People who are in trouble need God. God says he will save them. He sent Jesus to keep these promises. Jesus came to the world because people were in trouble and needed help. We each have different troubles at different times. However, we all will have the same trouble at one time. We all will die. Jesus came to die for us. He takes away our guilt. He keeps God's promise to come to us when we are in trouble. He saves us.

Now all the glasses are filled. They don't need the pitcher any more. Sometimes when we are filled with God's blessings, we think we don't need him any more either. If you have no troubles, there's no reason to call him.

But listen to something else God says in this psalm: "Let the giving of thanks be your sacrifice to God; and give the Almighty all that you promised." God tells us we need him when we are in trouble, and we know that. But he also says we need him when we are filled with blessings. Do you know you also need God when everything is going great? You need God because you need someone to thank.

You know you can pour something to drink from the pitcher into the glass. It is also true that you can pour something from the glass back into the pitcher—or into another glass. (Demonstrate.) God gives us gifts, and we can give gifts back to God. The gifts always start with God. When he blesses us, we can thank him and serve him. You give gifts back to God when you thank him and worship him and when you tell others about him. You also worship God when you give gifts to others in his name.

When do you need God? You need him when you have a problem, because you need help. You need him when you don't have a problem, because you need to thank him.

Who Is Invited?

Sing to the Lord, all the world!
Worship the Lord with joy;
come before him with happy songs!
Never forget that the Lord is God.
He made us, and we belong to him;
we are his people, we are his flock.
Psalm 100:1-3 (Fourth Sunday after Pentecost)

Several copies of the above psalm for each child. If possible duplicate the psalm in the form of an invitation

---

This *(show copy of psalm)* is an invitation. God is having a party. He is inviting people to come to his place. God knows how to have a good party. He says those who come will be happy and filled with joy. They are invited to sing and to have fun.

God's party sounds great. However, before you can go, you need an invitation. Do you think God has invited you to his party? Your name is not on this invitation. But look what the invitation does say. It says, "Sing to the Lord, all the world!" The invitation is sent to *all the world*—to everyone who has ever lived, who is alive now, and who ever will live. Later the psalm also says, "[God] made us, and we belong to him; we are his people, we are his flock." God invites everyone he created—and he created all people. We all belong to him, because he is the only God and we are all his people.

God made us all, and he still loves us all. The Bible says, "For God loved the world so much that he gave his only Son" (John 3:16). Jesus died for the sins of the

78

world. He offers forgiveness to everyone. After he rose from the dead, Jesus told his disciples, "Go, then, to all peoples everywhere and make them my disciples" (Matt. 28:19). God loves all people, Jesus died for all people, and he wants all people to know it.

So each of you gets an invitation. *(Give a copy of the psalm to each child.)* You are invited to God's party. His party starts now and will last forever. You can enjoy being with God now because he has come to be with you. You can enjoy being with him forever because he will take you to heaven.

Now that you have an invitation to God's party, think about one more thing. You can go to the party. But what about your family and friends? They are also a part of this world. God wants them to be invited too. When you get the invitation to God's party, it is not for you alone. You can invite others too. You can pass your invitation on to someone else. I'll even give you extra invitations. See the part that says, "all the world" and the part that says, "He made us, and we belong to him." You can give this invitation to others and tell them God wants them at his party too. If you run out of these printed invitations, you can still invite others to be with God. Tell them Jesus loves them and wants them to be his guests.

Learn to Get by Giving

THE WORD

[God,] My devotion to your Temple
burns in me like a fire;
the insults which are hurled at you fall on me.
Psalm 69:9 (Fifth Sunday after Pentecost)

THE WORLD

Ten dollars and coupons from a fast-food restaurant

Dan wanted to do something special for his family. He found these coupons from a restaurant in the newspaper. With the coupons and 10 dollars he could take his family out for hamburgers. So he mowed two lawns and earned 10 dollars. Then he took the family out to dinner.

While the family was enjoying the hamburgers, Dan thought about how hard he had worked to earn the 10 dollars. He told the others how hot it had been, how big the yards were, and how much trouble he had with the lawnmower. He did all the work for them.

His father said, "Dan, we thank you for working hard. We are glad you wanted to give something to us. Your mother and I also work so we can give you meals."

Then Dan thought about all the meals and other things his family gave him. He had worked hard for only one meal; they had to work for everything. Because he had learned to give, he had also learned something about what he received from others.

King David learned that same lesson. David loved God and wanted to do good things for God. He said, "My devotion to your Temple burns in me like a fire." David was eager to serve God. He wanted to worship in the temple. He wanted to give sacrifices. He wanted to bring others to the temple. Just as Dan wanted to do something for his family, David wanted to serve God.

Because David loved God, some people laughed at him. They thought it was funny that a king would go to the temple to worship. When people were angry at God, they would blame David by saying, "Your God didn't help me." David said to God, "The insults which are hurled at you fall on me." David did not understand. He loved God and served him; yet he got into trouble. He was like Dan. Dan told his family how hard he worked to make the money to buy their dinner. David told God how much he served him and yet he had problems.

Because Dan worked to give something to his family, he learned how much more his family gave him. David also learned that when he gave things to God, he also could understand how much more God had given him. God loved David, as he loves us all. He sent Jesus to be the Savior of the world. David had some insults put on him, because he served God. But Jesus had all the insults and all the sins of the world put on him, because he loved us.

I hope you are like David and want to serve God. Your love for God can burn like a fire in you—that is, he makes you want to worship him and serve him. People may laugh at you when you serve Jesus. You may have to give up other things that would be fun to do. However, when you give up something for Jesus, you will learn what he gave up for you. When Dan paid for one meal, he understood how much more his parents did for him. When you serve God, you will discover how much more God serves you.

Forever Is a Long Time

THE WORD

You said, "I have made a covenant with a man I chose;
I have promised my servant David,
'A descendant of yours will always be king;
I will preserve your dynasty forever.' "
                    Psalm 89:3-4 (Sixth Sunday after Pentecost)

THE WORLD

Enough building blocks to make a stack that will fall over, and a pole at least five feet long

---

When David was the king of Israel, he started a dynasty. Let me show you what a dynasty is. This block is King David. He was the first king of the dynasty. His son Solomon was the next king. He is the next block. *(Put another block on top of the first.)* Solomon's son Rehoboam became the next king. *(Add a block.)* His son was the next king and his son the next. *(Continue to add blocks as you speak until the stack falls over.)* A dynasty is the rule of many kings, each one the son of his father before him.

David and Solomon were good kings, but some of their descendants were bad. They worshiped false gods. They did other evil things and would not repent. The dynasty became shaky. About 400 years after it started, the last part of the great nation of Israel was destroyed. The dynasty was ended. The descendants of King David were no longer rulers of Israel.

God had promised King David that his descendants would always be kings. The promise is in Psalm 89, [The Lord] said, "I have made a covenant with the man I chose; I have promised my servant David, 'A descendant of yours will always be king; I will preserve your dynasty forever.' "

The psalm says David's dynasty will last forever. Forever is a long time. David's family did serve as kings longer than most dynasties, but 400 years is not forever. We know that when we stack one block on another the stack cannot go up forever. It will fall over. When one generation builds on another, we know it will not go on forever. Rich families will become poor. Powerful families will become weak.

But the promise in the psalm is true. David's family still has a descendant who is king. His dynasty still lasts today. David's dynasty does not depend on how good or how bad all those kings of Israel and Judah were. One special person was born into David's family. That person was Jesus. Jesus lived not as a king but as a carpenter. Yet he proved he was a king when he destroyed the power of sin and death by dying on a cross. He won a battle no other king had ever won. He destroyed death by rising from the grave.

Jesus was not just one king in a long dynasty of kings. He is the king who rules forever. He is like this pole. I cannot build a stock of blocks this high. They would fall over. But Jesus is the one and only king. He was the king long ago. He is the king now. He will be king forever. His rule will not fall, because it is built on his victory over death.

Jesus is king forever. Forever is a long time. We do not have to worry that his rule will end. His rule does not depend on how good his descendants are, as David's rule did. Because Jesus rose from the dead, he is the king who lives forever. He is the king we worship and serve today.

Who Gets God's Help?

The Lord is faithful to his promises,
and everything he does is good.
He helps those who are in trouble;
he lifts those who have fallen.
Psalm 145:13b-14 (Seventh Sunday after Pentecost)

THE WORLD
Two examples of children's art: one neatly done and showing artistic talent, the other sloppy and without merit

---

Tommy and Jerry were bored and told their mother they didn't have anything to do. She found an art class for them at the city park. Neither boy knew much about art, but since they had nothing else to do, they went to the classes.

On the first day in the class Tommy drew this picture *(hold up good one)* and Jerry drew this one *(show poor one)*. As the teacher went through the pictures done by all the children, he stopped when he saw Tommy's work. He could tell that Tommy was a good artist. Even though he had not taken lessons before, he had natural talent. When the teacher saw Jerry's picture, he thought that Jerry had no talent and perhaps no interest in art.

Which boy would the teacher help most? It depends on the teacher. One teacher might think: *I'll help Tommy. He has talent. He is interested in art. With some help Tommy can become a great artist. There is no reason to waste time on Jerry. He has no talent. He will never be an artist.* But another teacher might think: *I'll help Jerry. He needs a lot of help. He'll never be an artist, but I can*

84

help him do better, and he can learn to enjoy the art work that others do. Tommy already has talent. He can learn on his own.

We often think of Jesus as a teacher. Which kind of a teacher is he? Is he one who would help Tommy because Tommy has talent? Or would he help Jerry because he needs more help. Jesus is not an art teacher. He teaches us the way of life—life here on earth and the life which will last forever in heaven.

Just as Jerry had problems when he drew his picture, we often have problems as we live our lives on this earth. We do things that are wrong, things that hurt ourselves and others. We have problems that we have made and problems that others have made for us. Sometimes we feel like giving up. Jerry must have thought: *I can't draw, I might as well quit.* Sometimes we think: *I'm so bad I'll never go to heaven. Why should I even try to be good.*

We can try because Jesus is our teacher. He is the kind of teacher who helps those who need help the most. Listen to how our psalm describes the way God thinks about people who need help. It says, "The Lord is faithful to his promises, and everything he does is good. He helps those who are in trouble; he lifts those who have fallen."

Jesus did not come to earth to search for good people. He knew all of us have sinned. He knew all of us need his help. So he gave his life to pay for all sin. He came to be with people who have troubles, with those who have fallen. When you feel bad about yourself, remember Jesus came to help those who need help. When someone you know is sad and afraid, tell that person that Jesus came to help him too.

A Place Where Everyone Meets

THE WORD

People everywhere will come to you
on account of their sins.
Our faults defeat us,
but you forgive them.

> Psalm 65:2b-3 (Eighth Sunday after Pentecost)

THE WORLD

The numbers 1 through 7 each printed on a separate piece of paper and taped where they can be seen around the room; the following equations each written on a piece of paper: $1 + 4 =$, $2 + 3 =$, $5 + 0 =$, $6 - 1 =$, $7 - 2 =$, $8 - 3 =$, $5 - 0 =$

Can you find the numbers 1 through 7 in this room. *(Help the children locate each number in order, by having a child stand by each number. Then ask the children to come back together again.)*

Now I am going to give each of you a math assignment. Each of these pieces of paper has an equation for you to work. Do not tell me the answer. Instead, go to the number that is the correct answer and stand by it. *(Hand out the papers. Help any child who might have difficulties.)*

Look—all of you are standing by the same number. Does that mean each of you had the same equation? No, each of you was given a different problem to solve. But all the different problems had the same answer. All of you were right when you chose five as your answer.

Just as each of you had a different math equation, people also have different problems. Some are worried. Some are sick. Some are hungry. Some are afraid. But there is one problem that all people have. We all have the problem of sin and guilt. We have all done things that we should not have done. None of us has done all the things we should have done. We each may have different sins, just as I gave each of you different math problems. But the answer to all the sins is the same. The only answer to sin is Jesus. Jesus is the only person who was holy and without sin. He is also the only one who died to pay for everyone else's sin.

Because God sent Jesus to be our Savior from sin, we all need to go to God through Jesus. Just as all of you went to the number five as the answer to your different equations, all of us go to Jesus for forgiveness from our sins.

Even way back before Jesus was born, King David knew that God would forgive him. He knew God had promised a Savior. So David said, "People everywhere will come to you on account of their sins. Our faults defeat us, but you forgive them."

Look at all the people who are here today. Some of the people have other problems too, and we know God will also help them with the other problems. But all of us have the problem of sin. All of us confess our sin. And God forgives us all.

When we refuse to admit we have done wrong, sin keeps us away from each other. But when we confess our sins to God, we all come together in one place to receive his forgiveness through Jesus Christ.

Another Way Out

THE WORD

Proud men are coming against me, O God;
a gang of cruel men is trying to kill me—
people who pay no attention to you.
But you, O Lord, are a merciful and loving God,
always patient, always kind and faithful.

Psalm 86:14-15 (Ninth Sunday after Pentecost)

THE WORLD

A strong rope

King David had a problem. He said, "Proud men are coming against me, O God; a gang of cruel men is trying to kill me—people who pay no attention to you." David was afraid. A gang of cruel men wanted to kill him. He had a right to be scared. He knew that not even God could tell them to leave him alone, because they would not listen to God.

David felt as this girl does when I tie a rope around her. *(Tie the rope around a child. Make it loose enough so the child can slip out.)* When I have this rope around her, I can drag her everywhere I want to take her. Are you strong enough to get away? *(Encourage girl to pull on the rope.)* See, the rope is too strong. She can't break it.

David knew he could not defend himself from the cruel men. They were strong—like this rope. David could have said, "God is stronger than the gang of men. He will use his power to destroy them. My God is stronger than they are." But David did not say that. What would happen if I put another, even stronger, rope over this girl and pulled the other way? She would be hurt. When one group tries to prove it is stronger than another, many people get hurt.

But David did not try to match God's power against the cruel men. Instead, he said, "But you, O Lord, are a merciful and loving God, always patient, always kind and faithful." God is powerful, but David did not depend on God's power. Instead, he depended on God's mercy, love, patience, and kindness. When David felt the strong men coming against him, he did not try to fight strength with strength. Instead, he depended on God's love and kindness—for himself and for the cruel men.

God protected David by his love and kindness. David had found another way out. This girl couldn't break the rope to get free, but she also has another way out. *(Let the other children help her discover that she can slip out of the rope.)* See, you are free from the rope—not because you could break it, but because you found another way out.

We are weak and cannot use power to fight against all the problems of sin and guilt, but God has given us another way out. He sent Jesus to be with us. Jesus came to fight against sin, but he did not use his power against people who sin. He did not attack and kill anyone. He had another way out. He died to pay for all sins. He showed us that David was right: God is a merciful and loving God, always patient, always kind and faithful. By giving us his kindness and mercy, he gives us a way to escape from sin and death.

Know Where to Look

THE WORD
Your teachings are wonderful;
I obey them with all my heart.
The explanation of your teachings gives light
and brings wisdom to the ignorant.
Psalm 119:129-130 (Tenth Sunday after Pentecost)

THE WORLD
Hide a balloon (or piece of gum, fruit, etc.) for each
child in a large box along with newspapers, smaller
boxes, and toys. Place the large box where it cannot
be seen

I have a balloon for each of you. It is hidden some-
place in this room. You can have it—if you find it. Where
do you think your balloon is? *(Suggest some of the places
where the balloons might be and give the children the
opportunity to name more places.)* You will have a hard
time finding your balloon.

Let me give you a clue. The balloons are hidden in this
box. You still have to look for your balloon to find it, but
now you know where to look. *(Allow the children to look
through the things in the box and find the balloons. Give
each child one.)*

I have another gift for you that is much more important
than a balloon. This special gift is not from me. It is from
God. God wants to give you his love. He wants to be
with you. He wants to give you himself. But how will
you find God? How can you be sure he loves you?

Some people search all over the world to find God's
love. They may look in nature to find God's love, but
they also find storms and earthquakes. They may look at

good health to find God's love, but they also find sickness and death. They may look for happiness to find God's love, but they also find sadness. Looking all over the world for God's love is like searching this entire room to find one little balloon.

The psalm for today gives us a clue. It says, "Your teachings are wonderful; I obey them with all my heart. The explanation of your teachings gives light and brings wisdom to the ignorant."

You found the balloons when I gave you the clue to look in the box. The psalm gives us a clue to help us find God's love. It says we should look at God's teachings. God does not want to hide from you. He gives us his teachings in the Bible so we can read and hear them.

When you searched through the box, you found the balloons I had for you. When you search through the Bible, you find the love God has for you. God's teachings in the Bible show God's love for us. He gave us that love when he sent his Son Jesus to be the Savior of the world. Jesus loves us so much that he died to take away our sins. But God's teachings tell us that Jesus is still alive. He came back from the dead to live forever— and through him we can live forever too.

When you need God's love, remember where to look. Search the Bible to find Jesus and see how he loves you.

Know Where to Look for Help

THE WORD

All of them depend on you
to give them food when they need it.
You give it to them, and they eat it;
you provide food, and they are satisfied.
> Psalm 104:27-28 (Eleventh Sunday after Pentecost)

THE WORLD

A pet's dish and a box of pet food

Maybe some of you have a pet cat or dog. If so, you probably have a dish like this. Your pet depends on you for food. Your pet knows that you put the food in the dish. So when it is hungry, it looks for the dish. If the dish is here, the pet comes here and waits for you to bring the food. If the dish is here *(move it to another place)*, the pet comes here.

The psalm for today says that all the animals, birds, and fish are like your pet. They go to where the food is. All creatures need to eat. They will move from place to place to have enough to eat, just as your pet will go to where its dish is. The psalm writer says to God, "All of them depend on you to give them food when they need it. You give it to them, and they eat it; you provide food, and they are satisfied." God feeds the animals, birds, and fish. They all go to the place where God provides the food.

That psalm not only discribes the animals, birds, and fish; it also describes us. We also go to the place where the food is. When you are hungry, you are eager to get home, because you know your parents will give you food.

When Jesus lived on earth, people who were hungry came to him and he fed them. After they ate the food, many of them received something far more than the food they had eaten. Some of them wondered: *Why does Jesus give us food to eat and not make us pay for it?* They listened to Jesus and learned why he fed them. He loved them. He wanted to help them. Some wondered: *How can Jesus feed many people when he only has a little food for himself?* They watched him and saw the answer. Jesus had the power to feed them because he was God. They learned they could depend on Jesus—not just for food. They could depend on him to help them in all their needs. As they listended to him and watched him, they learned that he was their Savior. They saw him die to pay for their sins. They saw him after he came back to life again. They wanted to stay with him.

You can learn something from your pet. Move your pet's dish around and watch how it will follow the dish because it knows where to go to get food. The pet depends on you for help. You depend on Jesus to help you. Your pet knows to go to the dish to get food. You can learn to go to church and to be with other Christians, where you will receive the gifts Jesus has for you.

Learn where to go to find Jesus. Read about him in the Bible. Listen to others who tell you about the Savior who has forgiven your sins. You can depend on Jesus. When you are with him, you will be satisfied.

Who Speaks First?

THE WORD

Man's loyalty will reach up from the earth,
and God's righteousness will look down from heaven.

Psalm 85:11 (Twelfth Sunday after Pentecost)

THE WORLD

A strong magnet and a hacksaw blade (or other thin but visible piece of metal)

When you and I meet, we both say "Hi." As long as we are friends, we don't worry about who speaks first. However, before we knew each other, we didn't speak to one another. We often walk past people we do not know without saying a word. Or sometimes people who know each other get angry. When they meet, each wonders if the other will speak. Often when people have a misunderstanding, each thinks the other should speak first.

Now think about you and God. You know God; he knows you. He sent his Son Jesus to be one of us. Jesus is our friend. Because we know Jesus, we know God. That means we can talk to God and God can talk to us. We talk to each other in our worship. We hear God speak to us through his Word. We speak to him in our prayers and our songs.

Sometimes we do not feel like talking to God, because we have done wrong. We have said and done bad things. We wonder whether or not we can talk to God. I hope you never feel this way, but some people are afraid to come to church because they think God is angry at them and won't speak to them.

That's why I want to read Psalm 85, verse 11 to you.

It says, "Man's loyalty will reach up from the earth, and God's righteousness will look down from heaven."

This psalm tells us how we reach out to God and how God reaches out to us. It says we are *loyal,* that means *faithful,* to God. We reach out to God when we trust him. The psalm also says God sends righteousness down to us. Jesus came to earth to give us his goodness. He was perfect for us. God reaches out through Jesus and gives us his righteousness.

Which happens first? Are we first loyal to God and then he gives us his righteousness? Or does he first give us his righteousness and then we are loyal to him? Does he speak to us first? Or do we speak to him first?

I'll show you something to help answer those questions. This is a magnet. It has a power that we can't see. It will pick up metal. See how the blade is pulled to the magnet. *(Demonstrate.)* The two come together, because the power in the magnet pulls the blade to itself.

The magnet is like God. He has a gift of love for each of us. The power starts in God. We are like the blade. When we feel God's power, we are pulled to him, just as the blade is pulled to the magnet. The blade does not have the power to move to the magnet unless the magnet gives it the power. We cannot be loyal to God unless he gives us his righteousness. God speaks to us first so we can speak to him. The Bible says we love God because he first loved us.

I hope you feel close to God. If you ever feel far away from him, or if you know someone else who feels far from him, remember the magnet, the blade, and this psalm. God will always speak to us first. He will give us his goodness and love. Then we can move to him, because he has reached out to us.

A Gift for You—and Others

THE WORD

God, be merciful to us and bless us;
look on us with kindness,
so that the whole world may know your will;
so that all nations may know your salvation.
Psalm 67:1-2 (Thirteenth Sunday after Pentecost)

THE WORLD

A pencil (or other item used in school) for each child

School starts soon. Many of you are getting new clothes, crayons, and books to go back to school. Even the children who are too young for school like to have school supplies like their older brothers and sisters.

(Choose one boy from the group.) I will help you get ready to go back to school. I have a pencil for you. It is a brand new pencil with an eraser. You can use it to do your schoolwork. I hope you enjoy the pencil.

Now for the rest of you. I gave this boy a pencil. Of course, you need a pencil just as much as he does. You could also use it at school or at home. Since I gave him a pencil, do you think I will give you one too?

I will read a part of Psalm 67 to you, and from these words I want you to figure out if I will give you a pencil or not.

The psalm says, "God, be merciful to us and bless us; look on us with kindness. . . ." First, let's talk about that much of the psalm; then I will read the rest. The people of Israel were asking God to bless them and to be kind to them. They wanted God to love them and forgive them. They wanted his help. We will pretend this boy is the people of Israel. He needed a pencil, and I gave one to

96

him. The children of Israel needed God's help, and God gave it to them.

Now listen to what else the psalm says. ". . .so that the whole world may know your will; so that all nations may know your salvation." The people of Israel said that if God blessed them, all the other people in the world would see the blessing. The other people would then come to God and ask for the same gift. Since God had given salvation to the Israelites, he would give it to the others too.

None of you came here to get a pencil. But since I gave this boy one, all of you want one too. So I will give each of you a pencil. *(Distribute the pencils.)*

Now I want to give you another gift. Jesus loves you. He is your Savior, because he died for you and he rose from the dead. He lives with you now. This gift is the salvation promised to all nations in the psalm we read today. Because Jesus came to the people of Israel, he has come to us and we have received his blessing too.

You may take the pencil to school. I do not have a pencil to give to each of your classmates. However, we do have a more important gift for everyone. Tell and show others that God loves you and helps you. When others see your gift from God, they will want it too. God will give his blessings to everyone.

When God Reaches Down

THE WORD

Even though you are so high above,
you care for the lowly,
and the proud cannot hide from you.

> Psalm 138:6 (Fourteenth Sunday after Pentecost)

THE WORLD

A rope at least six feet long

(Stand near a child who is sitting down.) Do you think I can pull you up? *(Ask other children if they think you can pull the child from his seat.)* Okay, let's try. *(Take the child's hand and lift him.)* That was easy. You may sit back down.

(Move about six feet away from the child.) Do you think I can pull him up from here? *(Reach your arm out toward him to show you cannot reach him. Ask the children for their opinions.)*

Even though I can't reach him with my hand from here, I can still pull him up. Here, hold on to this. *(Throw one end of the rope to him.)* Now even though I am standing far away, I can pull him up. *(Pull on the rope until he stands.)*

When you feel God is close to you, you know that he can help you. *(Walk back to be near the child.)* When God is beside you, you know he loves you and helps you in all your needs. But sometimes we do not feel God close to us. God is great and powerful. He is God of all the world and of all the sky. Because he is so great and so holy, sometimes we feel he is far away from us.

We also feel God is far away from us when we know

we have sinned and do not deserve to be with him. When we do bad things, we sometimes want to hide from God, even though that is the time we need him most of all.

When God is far away, it often seems to us that he cannot help us. You knew I could pull this boy up when I stood near him, but you didn't think I could pull him up when I was far away. Just as I had a way to pull him up when I used the rope, God has a way to reach us even when he seems far away. Listen to what Psalm 138 says about God, "Even though you are so high above, you care for the lowly, and the proud cannot hide from you."

Even though God is great and powerful, he still loves all people. God found a way to reach down to us with his power. He sent his Son Jesus to be our Savior. Jesus is like the rope. I could use my strength to pull this boy up by pulling on the rope. In the same way God can use his power to help us by giving that power to Jesus. Jesus came to be with us. He brings God's power to us. Even if we try to hide from God, Jesus comes to be with us.

Remember that God always cares about you. He wants to reach out to help you. No matter how great and powerful God is, he has time for you and he wants to help you.

Before and After

THE WORD
> Declare me innocent, O Lord,
> because I do what is right and trust you completely.
> Examine me and test me, Lord;
> judge my desires and thoughts.
> Your constant love is my guide;
> your faithfulness always leads me.
>> Psalm 26:1-3 (Fifteenth Sunday after Pentecost)

THE WORLD
> Two dinner plates, one clean and the other covered with messy food

Tell me what you see. *(Show the dirty plate.)* Do you like what you see? Would you eat a meal from this plate? Now tell me what you see. *(Show the clean plate.)* Would you eat a meal from this plate?

These two plates could be the same one. This one is the plate before it is washed. This could be the same plate after it is washed. You would not want to eat from the dirty plate as it is now. But if it were washed, it would look like this clean plate, and you'd be glad to eat from it. How you see the plate depends on whether you look at it before or after it is washed.

When King David tells us about himself, he says he looks like both of these plates. First, he said this about himself, "I have been evil from the time I was born; from the day of my birth I have been sinful." (Ps. 51:5). King David said he was like the dirty plate. He had said and done bad things.

But he also said this about himself, "Declare me innocent, O Lord, because I do what is right and trust you completely. Examine me and test me, Lord; judge my desires and thoughts." David also says he is a good person who does what is right. He says he is like the clean plate.

Which is the real King David? Is he a bad sinner? Is he a good person? He is both. By himself he is a sinner—like the dirty plate. However, he is not by himself. God is with him. David said to God, "Your constant love is my guide; your faithfulness always leads me." God was with David and helped him. God washed away his sin, so David became like the clean plate. Without God David was a sinful person. With God he was forgiven.

You and I are also like both plates. By ourselves we know we are sinners. We have said and done things that hurt ourselves and others. But God sent Jesus to help us. Jesus washed away our sin and made us clean. When we were baptized, we were washed in Jesus' name. Each day he cleans us again and again, just as we wash the plates after every meal.

When you feel bad about yourself and think you are like this dirty plate, remember what Jesus has done for you. He died to take away your sin. He has made you clean again.

Other people who do bad things look like the dirty plate. But remember Jesus died for them too. You can tell them about Jesus, and they will be forgiven too.

Change What You Want

Give me the desire to obey your laws
rather than to get rich.
Psalm 119:36 (Sixteenth Sunday after Pentecost)

THE WORLD
A red card with a 5 on it, a green card with a 4 on it,
a white card with $2 + 3 =$ and another with $2 + 2 =$

We often want the wrong things. We want things that
seem as if they will be fun, but when we get them, they
hurt us. Sometimes you ask your mother or father for
something, and your parent says you can't have it because
it's not good for you. You may want food that would be
bad for you. You may want to do something that would
be dangerous.

One of the most important lessons you can learn for
your life on this earth is how to want the right things. If
you learn to want things that will help you, if you work
for them, if you pray for them, you can have a good and
happy life. But if you want things that hurt you, if you
work for them, and even pray for them, you will have
many problems.

The psalm for today is a prayer. It asks God to help us
want the right things. It says, "Give me the desire to obey
your laws rather than to get rich." Whoever wrote the
psalm knew God loved him. He knew that if he could learn
to want the things God wanted him to have, he would be
happy. So he asked God to help him want the good things.

I hope this illustration will help you learn how to want
good things. Let's pretend green *(show card with 4)* is
good for you. Also pretend red *(show card with 5)* is

bad for you. Green will make you healthy and happy. Red will make you hurt and be sad.

Now look at this card. It says $3 + 2 =$. This is what is inside you. It is what you want. But $3 + 2 = 5$. The correct answer is on the red card. That makes you want red, but red is bad for you. We all want things that hurt us, because we are all sinners. What we want inside us adds up to things that hurt us. That is why we often choose things that hurt us. When we tell lies, hate someone, say bad things, or do other wrong things, they add up to cause problems for us and for others. We want what is bad.

We cannot change the red card. We cannot make bad into good. But we can change what we want. We can change this card, which says $3 + 2 =$, to this card, which says $2 + 2 =$. Now the correct answer is 4. The right answer is on the green card, and green is good for you. What you want leads you to something good.

When we want bad things, we cannot change the bad into good. But we can change what we want. We can change, because God answers the prayer in this psalm. We pray, "Give me the desire to obey your laws." God answered that prayer by sending Jesus to be our Savior. Jesus loves us and forgives our sins. Because we are forgiven, we can change what we want. Instead of wanting bad things that hurt us, we can want good things that help us.

As long as we live, we will want to say and do bad things. That's why we need Jesus every day. Ask him to help you change what you want. You can want good things instead of bad, because Jesus is good and he gives you his goodness. He wants to help you.

Jesus, the Garbage Man

THE WORD

[The Lord] does not punish us as we deserve
or repay us for our sins and wrongs. . . .
As far as the east is from the west,
so far does he remove our sins from us.
  Psalm 103:10, 12 (Seventeenth Sunday after Pentecost)

THE WORLD

A sack lunch, a sack of garbage, a large piece of
cardboard

This is a sack lunch. The sack is filled with good things
to eat. I'd like you to think of this as being the good things
in your life. Pretend it is love, faith, fun, happiness. Life
includes good things.

Your life also includes things that are not good. When
you make a lunch of good things, you may also have to
have some bad things. The bad things are in this sack of
garbage. Here is the spoiled fruit, the raw fat from meat,
the moldy bread. Think of this sack as the bad things in
your life. Pretend it is sin, guilt, worry, pain.

To have the good things in life, like a sack lunch, you
also have to have some bad things, like garbage. Sometimes the bad things ruin the good things. Would you
like to sit down at a table to eat your lunch and find the
garbage on the same table? Of course not. Many times we
cannot enjoy the good things that happen to us, because
the bad things are there at the same time.

But God has a way to help us. He helps us the same
way he helped David a long time ago. David said, "[The
Lord] does not punish us as we deserve or repay us for

our sins and wrongs. As far as the east is from the west, so far does he remove our sins from us."

God does not punish us as we deserve. He does not make us eat the garbage. He does not push our face in it. He doesn't make us feel bad about ourselves. Instead of punishing us for our sins, God takes our sin away from us. *(Move the garbage far away from the food.)* He takes the bad things far away from us so we can enjoy the good. David says, "As far as the east is from the west, so far does he remove our sins from us."

How far do you think the east is from the west? East is *(mention an area that is regarded as far east from your location)* and west is *(identify a place known as west).* God has taken your sin as far away as the east is from the west, as far as _____ is from _____.

But east and west can also be close. Pretend this cardboard is a wall. *(Put the grabage on one side and the food on the other.)* The garbage is east and the food is west, but they are close together. I would not mind eating my food here with the garbage there, as long as the wall is there.

This wall is like Jesus. Jesus separates us from our sin. He came into our lives and hauled the garbage away when he died for us. We have both good and bad in our lives. *(Put the bags together.)* But Jesus came to our side to take the bad away. *(Move the grabage back to the other side.)* Jesus is the garbage collector who takes our sin away. Then he comes back to be on our side to enjoy the good he has given us. We enjoy the good with him.

Help That Won't Quit

THE WORD

Don't be angry with me;
don't turn your servant away.
You have been my help;
don't leave me, don't abandon me,
O God, my savior.
My father and mother may abandon me,
but the Lord will take care of me.
　　　　Psalm 27:9b-10 (Eighteenth Sunday after Pentecost)

THE WORLD

A child and, if practical, some of the adults mentioned
in the message

David was a great king. He had someone to help him
with every problem. He had soldiers and bodyguards to
protect him. He had teachers and advisers to tell him what
to do. He had lots of money and people to manage it.
But most of all David knew God would help him.

David did not depend on his soldiers, his advisers, or
his money. He trusted in God. He knew that all the power
of any army, the wisdom of the wisest people and all the
riches in the world could not solve his problems. He was
a sinner; he had done wrong. Only God could remove sin.

David said, "Don't be angry with me; don't turn your
servant away. You have been my help; don't leave me,
don't abandon me, O God, my savior. My father and my
mother may abandon me, but the Lord will take care of
me." He knew that all the others who helped him, even
his mother and father, could not take away his sin. He
needed God.

Each of you also has many people to help you. *(Select*

one child from the group.) Will you come and help show how many people help each of us? How old are you? Okay, let's make this place where you are standing your age right now. You will walk in that direction and pretend you get older with each step.

First, let's think of the people who help you now. *(Let the children name those who help: parents, teachers, friends, doctors, babysitters, etc. They may name Jesus. If not, include him.)* Let's pretend these people are standing here *(or actually have them stand with the child).* You have all these people to help you today.

Now take one step forward. You are now 12 years old. Another step: you are 15; another step, and you are 20. Will you still have the same people helping you when you are 20? *(Name those who have dropped out or been replaced. Name those still with the child.)*

As this child gets older, others who have helped will no longer be here. As David said, even parents will abandon us. That doesn't mean they don't still love us, but they can help us only so much and only for so long. Every person who helps has limits. Teachers can teach only so much. Doctors can cure only so much. The police can prevent only so many accidents.

As each of you gets older and has fewer people to help you, you need not be afraid. Remember, David knew that God would not abandon him. God would stay with him.

God will also stay with you. He has sent his Son Jesus to live with you. Jesus helps you today. He loves you, and he helps you love others. He forgives you, and he helps you forgive others. He leads you through life. When others come to the limit of their ability to help, Jesus stays with you. He won't quit. He went right through death for you. After he died, he rose again. Now he goes through life with you. Even death can not make him leave you or you leave him.

Which Teacher Do You Want?

THE WORD

Teach me your ways, O Lord;
make them known to me.
Teach me to live according to your truth,
for you are my God, who saves me.
I always trust in you.

Psalm 25:4-5 (Nineteenth Sunday after Pentecost)

THE WORLD

A cassette player with three kinds of piano music *(see below)* on a tape

Would you like to learn how to play the piano? If you did, who would you ask to be your teacher? You could ask your father to teach you. It would be fun to be with him, and you could learn at home. Or maybe there is a nice teenager who lives next door. She is fun, and you like being with her. If she taught you, your parents wouldn't have to take you to lessons. You could walk. Which one would you choose: your father or the teenager.

Maybe you'd better listen to each of them play first. This is how the teenager plays the piano *(play tape of random banging on keys with no tune)*. The teenager may be a good friend, but I don't think she could teach you to play the piano.

This is your father at the piano *(play tape of a poor rendition of "Twinkle, Twinkle, Little Star")*. At least he knows the black keys from the white ones, but he is not ready to teach you how to play either.

Now listen to this *(play interesting tune, well played.)* That was by a piano teacher you don't even know. He lives two miles away and will charge you for lessons. But he knows how to play and how to teach. If you want to play the piano, you should take lessons from him.

Let's look for another kind of teacher—a teacher who will teach you how to enjoy your life on earth and then go to heaven. Where will you find such a teacher?

Maybe you know people who tell others to go to hell. Would you want such a person to teach you the way to heaven? That would be like having someone who didn't know how to play the piano try to teach you how to play. It won't work.

There are others who know the way to heaven. I do, but I still do wrong things. Your parents, Sunday school teacher, and others know the way to heaven, but they also do wrong things. All of us can teach you something. But we are like the father who could play, "Twinkle, Twinkle, Little Star." We need help in teaching you.

King David also wanted a teacher to show him how to be saved. He said, "Teach me your ways, O Lord; make them known to me. Teach me to live according to your truth, for you are my God, who saves me. I always trust in you." David asked God to be his teacher. God was the one who saved him, so he wanted God to teach him.

God also will be your teacher. He sent his Son Jesus to live on earth with us. Jesus first earned the way to heaven for you when he died to pay for your sins and rose from the dead to give you a life that will never end. Jesus is the teacher who knows the way from earth to heaven, because he came to earth, went through death, and then to heaven. When we believe in him, we follow him on earth and will follow him to heaven.

Jesus is the best teacher. He teaches you how to live here on earth, and he teaches the way to heaven. Your other teachers and I want to help you learn, but we want you to learn from Jesus.

The Vine Is Still Growing

THE WORD

You brought a grapevine out of Egypt;
you drove out other nations and planted it in their land.
You cleared a place for it to grow;
its roots went deep,
and it spread out over the whole land.
It covered the hills with its shade;
its branches overshadowed the giant cedars.
Psalm 80:8-10 (Twentieth Sunday after Pentecost)

THE WORLD

A house plant, preferably a vine

When God's people, the Israelites, left Egypt, they had been slaves. They went back to their own country and found other people living there. They had to fight wars to get their land back. They built homes and cities. They dug up the soil to plant crops. God blessed his people, and they became a great nation.

Psalm 80 tells how God helped them. It says, "You brought a grapevine out of Egypt; you drove out other nations and planted it in their land. You cleared a place for it to grow; its roots went deep, and it spread out over the whole land. It covered the hills with its shade; its branches overshadowed the giant cedars."

The psalm writer saw the people as though they were a plant like this. *(Show the children the plant.)* They were planted in one place, as this plant has its roots in the pot. But the plant grew and grew. Imagine this vine being like Jack's beanstalk. It grows out the door and down the street. It covers the whole town and reaches out into the country. The Israelites grew like that plant. They became a great nation, because their roots were in God. God gave them the power to grow. God protected them and blessed them. They used this psalm to thank God for his love and blessings.

Many years later God planted another vine on earth. Jesus is that vine. Because he is God, his roots reach to the power and love of God. He also became a person like us living on this earth. At first Jesus was a very small vine. At that time he suffered and died to pay for our sins. For three days everyone thought the vine was dead and gone. Then Jesus came back to life again. He told his followers to baptize all people in his name. People who believed in him became a part of the vine. Christ came into their lives, and they grew with him. The vine grew and grew.

Think of this vine when it was very little. It was like Jerusalem 2000 years ago. Then it started growing. Because it gets its power from God's love and mercy, it grew into Europe, Africa, and Asia. It grew for hundreds and now thousands of years. It came across to America. The vine now reaches around the world.

Because Jesus loves you and is your Savior, the vine has reached you. Because you believe in Jesus, you have become a part of the vine. Now you can reach out to others. Just as you have received God's love and forgiveness through others in the vine, you can also give God's love and forgiveness to others, because you are a part of the vine.

You Can Go Back to God

THE WORD
> You prepare a banquet for me,
> where all my enemies can see me;
> you welcome me as an honored guest
> and fill my cup to the brim.
> > Psalm 23:5 (Twenty-first Sunday after Pentecost)

THE WORLD
> A can of soft drink and a paper cup

After school Ginny and her friends often stopped by (*name a local convenience store*) to buy a treat. They all knew Mr. Landers who ran the store. He was their friend. One day Ginny was in an aisle in the store by herself. She took a can of peanuts and put it in her book bag. She didn't know why she did it, because she had enough money to buy the peanuts if she had wanted to.

When Ginny left the store with her friends, Mr. Landers asked her for the peanuts. He had seen her take them. All of her friends were afraid and ran away. Ginny was embarrassed. Mr. Landers talked to her about stealing. He told her she had hurt herself more than she had hurt him.

At school the next day Ginny's friends didn't talk to her much. She heard them whispering and thought they were talking about her. She felt alone. She didn't want to go to the store after school, but she didn't want to be alone either. So she tagged along with the others. She hoped Mr. Landers wouldn't see her.

When she came into the store, Mr. Landers called out, "Hi, Ginny, come here. I've got something for you." Mr. Landers poured Ginny's favorite drink into a cup (*do it*). He filled it to the brim. The others watched Ginny as she drank it. Then they came over and talked to her too. They knew Ginny and Mr. Landers were still friends, so they wanted to be Ginny's friend too.

King David felt that God treated him as Mr. Landers treated Ginny. David had done bad things, yet God was good to David. David said to God, "You prepare a banquet for me, where all my enemies can see me; you welcome me as an honored guest and fill my cup to the brim." David knew God had forgiven him, because he could see God still loved him.

Maybe you can also see yourself in the story about Mr. Landers and Ginny. When you do something wrong, you feel bad about yourself. You may also think other people are talking about you and won't like you. Sometimes when people feel guilty, they turn away from God. They don't go to church, don't pray, and don't read the Bible. But Ginny went back to the store, and Mr. Landers welcomed her. You can also go back to God, and he will welcome you. He will prepare a banquet for you so others can see he loves you. He will welcome you as an honored guest and fill your cup to the brim.

You know God loves you, because he sent Jesus to be your Savior. Jesus did not come to punish you for what you have done wrong. You do not need to hide from him. He came to forgive you. He took your punishment when he died for your sins. When he came back to life again, he went to heaven to prepare a place for you. Now he invites you to be with him.

How to Choose a Gift for God

THE WORD
> Praise the Lord's glorious name;
> bring an offering and come into his Temple.
> Bow down before the Holy One when he appears;
> tremble before him, all the earth!"
> Psalm 96:8-9 (Twenty-second Sunday after Pentecost)

THE WORLD
> A movie pass, a movie ticket, a five-dollar bill

Our psalm for today tells us to praise God and also how to do it. It says "Praise the Lord's glorious name; bring an offering and come into his Temple. Bow down before the Holy One when he appears; tremble before him, all the earth!"

We are here to praise God today. We are with God, because Jesus promised to be with us when we are gathered in his name. We bow before him in our acts of worship as we confess our sins and pray. We sing good things about him in songs. But what kind of an offering can we bring God? What can we give to God, who has everything?

I'll tell you a parable that may teach you how to choose a gift for God. An owner of a store wanted to thank all of his customers for shopping at his store. He rented a theater and arranged for a special movie. He gave each customer a pass, like this, to the movie. Those who had passes from the owner could see the movie for free.

One man who came to see the movie did not have a pass, but he had this ticket that he had bought. The usher at the theater told him he could not use the ticket that he had paid for. He needed a free pass. Then the man tried to give the usher this money. The usher refused the money.

He said he could let in only people who had the free passes from the owner.

God is like the store owner. He loves us and wants us to be with him. He invites us to worship him. He invites us to heaven. He gives us that invitation through his Son Jesus Christ. Jesus paid for our way to heaven when he suffered and died for us. He brought the invitation to us when he rose from the dead to give us a new life. Through Jesus, God has given us love and forgiveness. Those gifts are like the pass from the store owner.

When we come to worship God and when we go to heaven, we take the gift God gave to us and give it back to God. You may give love back to God in many ways. You may give money to help do God's work on earth. You may help people who are sick, lonely, or sad, just as Jesus helped such people. You may tell others that Jesus is their Savior. You may show kindness and love to people. In each of these ways you are giving back to God something that he gave you.

When you want to choose a gift for God, you do not take something that you think is yours, something you have made or earned, to give to God. You cannot be like the man who wanted to buy his way into the theater. Instead, you think about the gifts that God has given you. Any offering that you give to God is something that God has first given to you. When you return the gift, you are not saying you don't want or need it. Instead, you are praising God for giving you the gift. You are saying you know he will continue to give you more gifts. You are showing you love God and trust him.

The Law That Helps

THE WORD

Happy are those who reject the advice of evil men,
who do not follow the example of sinners
or join those who have no use for God.
Instead, they find joy in obeying the Law of the Lord,
and they study it day and night.
　　　　Psalm 1:1-2 (Twenty-third Sunday after Pentecost)

THE WORLD

A stop sign and a paper sign that slips over it, saying:
SPEED LIMIT 55

This stop sign was at a street corner where many children walked to school. Because of the sign, cars would stop and the children could cross the street safely. One day some children thought they would have fun by changing the sign. They slipped this paper over the stop sign. This makes the sign read: SPEED LIMIT 55.

The people who drove on that street every day knew the sign was there, so they stopped anyway. However, someone new in the neighborhood drove down the street. He saw no stop sign. He was driving slower than 55 miles per hour. As he came to the corner, some children were walking across the street. They thought the car would stop. The driver had to swerve to miss the children. He hit another car. Several people were hurt and had to go to the hospital.

The stop sign was put there to help people. When the children changed the sign, they caused people to get hurt. Our psalm for today tells us God's law has also been given to help us. It says, "Happy are those who find joy in obeying the Law of the Lord, and they study it day and night."

God's law helps us live together without hurting one another, just as traffic signs help people drive without having accidents.

The psalm also warns us not to follow those who change God's law. It says, "Happy are those who reject the advice of evil men, who do not follow the example of sinners or join those who have no use for God."

Sometimes people change God's law, just as the children changed the sign. God told us not to lie; we change his command if we say it's okay to tell some lies. God said to love all people; we change the law if we say we can love some people and can hate or ignore others. God said we are to love him; we change the law if we love other things more than God.

This psalm warns us not to change God's law and not to follow others who change it. Instead, we are to study God's law to see how he wants to help us. We are not afraid to read his law, even when it shows us we have not always obeyed it. The Bible also tells us that God sent his Son Jesus to be our Savior. Jesus suffered and died to take the punishment we deserve for breaking the law. He has obeyed the law for us.

God did not give us the law to hurt us, but to help us. If we change the law, we cannot receive God's help. But we do not have to change it, because Jesus has obeyed the law for us. He has saved us from being punished. When we know that God loves us and forgives us, we can be happy as we study his law.

I Need You, God

THE WORD

O God, you are my God,
and I long for you.
My whole being desires you;
like a dry, worn-out, and waterless land,
my soul is thirsty for you.

Psalm 63:1 (Twenty-fourth Sunday after Pentecost)

THE WORLD

A picture of water (a stream, lake, or waterfall), an empty glass, and a pitcher of water.

David wrote the psalm we use today when he was in a desert. A desert may be beautiful, but it is also dangerous for people. The plants and animals that live in deserts are able to live in hot places with very little water, but people need water often. If we get too hot, we get sick and can even die.

David was thirsty when he was in the desert. He remembered how good water is. What if he had had a picture like this? He could have looked at the cool water and pretended he was splashing in it. But the picture wouldn't help his thirst. Or David might have looked at an empty glass like this and remembered how often he had drunk water from it. But remembering water he had drunk last week would not help today. What he wanted and needed was water like this. *(Pour water into glass.)* He needed a cool drink.

When David was thirsty out in the desert, he also understood that he needed God even more than he needed water. The desert reminded him of his life. He felt alone and afraid. He had sinned and felt guilty. Just as his body needed water, his soul needed God's love. He said, "O God, you are my God, and I long for you. My whole being desires you; like a dry, worn-out, and waterless land, my soul is thirsty for you."

David did not want a statue of God, any more than he wanted a picture of water. He needed the real God. He did not want a reminder of what God had done a long time ago, any more than he wanted to see an empty glass to remind him of the water he drank last week. He wanted to be with God. He wanted to feel God's love and forgiveness. He wanted to worship God, to thank him and praise him.

David knew that God was with him and was as real as this glass of water. He knew God, who had helped him in the past, was still there. He knew God had promised that one of his descendents would be the Savior who would pay for the sins of the world. David knew he needed God as desert plants and animals need water. David also knew that God loved him and wanted to help him.

You and I also need God. We need him to help us when we have troubles. We need him to forgive our sins. We need him to love us. We need to love him and worship him.

God kept his promise to David and sent a Savior. Jesus is not just a picture of God. Jesus is God who became a person to live with us and to die for us. The stories about Jesus' death and resurrection from the dead are not just reminders of what happened long ago. They are not like the empty glass that we drank from last week. What Jesus did long ago is for us today. (Show pitcher of water.) When Jesus died for us long ago, he paid for our sin today. When he rose from the dead, he came back to live with people, and he is still with us today. He is like a fresh drink of water for our souls every day.

Be Wise Now

THE WORD
Teach us how short our life is,
so that we may become wise.
Psalm 90:12 (Twenty-fifth Sunday after Pentecost)

THE WORLD
An opaque bottle of shampoo, two transparent bottles
—one full and one almost empty

We often think that people who live a long time become very wise. So it may surprise you to hear the psalm
for today. It says, "Teach us how short our life is, so that
we may become wise."

The person who wrote this psalm thinks we need to be
wise because life is short. He says we shouldn't wait until
we get old to become wise. Wise up today, because you
may not be alive tomorrow. We may wonder why we need
to be wise if life is short. Why bother to learn something
today if we're not going to be living tomorrow?

Maybe these bottles will help us understand this psalm.
Look at these two bottles of shampoo *(show the opaque
and almost empty bottles)*. How much shampoo is in this
one? You can't see through the bottle, so you don't know
how much is in it. It could be full, or it could be empty.
But look at the other bottle. You can see it is almost empty.
When the shampoo gets that low in the bottle, you know
it is time to buy some more. But when you look at the other
bottle, you don't know when you need to buy more.

Our lives are like this bottle *(show the opaque one)*.
We don't know how much longer we will live. We may
have many years left in our lives. Or our lives may be
almost over. Since we don't know if we will live a long

time or a short time, we don't know how to prepare for the time we have to live.

The psalm writer asks God to make us wise. He says we should all learn that life is short. It is short, because we live only one day at a time. We never know how many more days or years we will live, so it is always short. But you don't have to be afraid because life is short. Instead, you can learn that life is short and learn to be wise about it.

What do you do when you see the shampoo bottle is almost empty? You buy a new bottle, of course. If your life is like this bottle *(show opaque one)* you do not know if it is almost gone. But if you are wise, you will go ahead and get a new bottle. If your life is short here on this earth and you are wise, you will get a new life.

Yet you can't go out and buy a new life as you buy a new bottle of shampoo. That's why you need to be wise. Know that Jesus Christ has bought a new life for you. Jesus became like an empty bottle. His life ended when he died on the cross. But that wasn't the end of him. He came back from death, and now he has a full life like this bottle *(show the full transparent one)*. He gives us this new life with him.

Don't worry about how long your life is to be on this earth. Be wise and know that Jesus has already given you a new life. Whenever your life here runs out, you already have a new one in heaven.

Check Your Faith Gauge

THE WORD

I am content and at peace.
As a child lies quietly in its mother's arms,
so my heart is quiet within me.
Israel, trust in the Lord now and forever!
Psalm 131:2-3 (Twenty-sixth Sunday after Pentecost)

THE WORLD

A large "Faith Gauge," like a gas gauge on a car, with
SCARED on the left side and SAFE on the right and a
movable needle

This is a "Faith Gauge." Let me show you how it works.
When I am scared, the needle points way over to this side
(demonstrate). That means my faith is low. When I feel
safe and secure, the needle points way over to this side
(demonstrate). That means I am full of faith.

Let's try the "Faith Gauge" on you. Pretend you are
walking down the street by yourself and a big dog comes
along. The dog barks and growls at you. What would
happen to your "Faith Gauge"? The needle would probably go way over to the side marked SCARED *(demonstrate)*. You would be afraid the dog might bite you.

But just then your father comes along and he holds
your hand. What happens? I think the needle would move
toward the middle. You know your father will protect
you, but you are still a little bit scared—and maybe he is
too. Now the owner of the dog comes and puts a leash
on him. He leads the dog away. You are still walking with
your hand in your father's. Now the needle would go way
over to SAFE *(demonstrate)*.

Think about a little baby that wakes up all alone. The

122

baby is afraid and cries. The needle goes over to SCARED. Then the mother picks up the baby and hugs it. The baby feels safe. The needle goes to the other side.

If each of us really had a "Faith Gauge," the needle would move back and forth many times a day. The psalm for today tells us how to keep the needle over on the side marked SAFE. It says: "I am content and at peace. As a child lies quietly in its mother's arms, so my heart is quiet within me. Israel, trust in the Lord now and forever!"

When David wrote this psalm, he was at peace; he was filled with faith. But David wasn't at peace all of the time. When he was in battle, he knew he could be killed. At other times he was not at peace, because he knew he had sinned and he felt guilty. Each time David remembered God was with him. He knew he could trust God to protect him. So David was at peace.

David tells you how you can be at peace too. We are all afraid sometimes. When you are afraid, think of this "Faith Gauge." It is called a "Faith Gauge" because it reminds you when you need to trust in the Lord. When you are afraid, remember Jesus promised to be with you always. Have faith in him, and you will be safe. When you know you have been wrong, remember Jesus died to pay for your sins. Trust Jesus to forgive you. Then you are safe. Your sins are gone.

Look at your "Faith Gauge" often. When your faith is low, remember the good news of Jesus Christ. He will give you peace. He will make you safe.

Be Glad You Belong to God

THE WORD

Be glad that we belong to [the Lord];
let all who worship him rejoice.
Go to the Lord for help,
and worship him continually.
Psalm 105:3-4 (Twenty-seventh Sunday after Pentecost)

THE WORLD

Two old stuffed toy animals—one dirty and torn, the other clean and having signs of repair

---

Last Christmas Billy and his brother Kevin each received a stuffed toy animal as a present. This is Billy's toy animal *(show the one that is clean and repaired)*. You can tell he has had it for a long time. It shows signs of wear, but it is clean, because Billy takes good care of it. He tries to keep it from getting dirty. When it is dirty, he washes it. It has been torn, but Billy always fixes it. See this place where he sewed the arm back in place.

This is Kevin's toy animal *(show the torn and dirty one)*. It is exactly the same age as Billy's, but look how dirty it is. Kevin never washes his toy. See how it is worn. An eye is missing. It is in bad shape, because Kevin never fixes his toy.

If you were a toy animal, would you rather belong to Billy or to Kevin? I'd rather belong to Billy because he takes care of his toys.

However, you are not a toy. You are a person. You belong to God. I'd like for you to think about what it means that you belong to God. You will see that God is like Billy. God takes care of those who belong to him. Listen to what our psalm for today says, "Be glad that we belong [to the Lord]; let all who worship him rejoice. Go to the Lord for help; and worship him continually."

You belong to God, because he created you. Be glad he created you. He made you to be a person, because he wants to love you and to take care of you. He wants to be with you.

Even though God created us, we have sinned and caused problems for ourselves. Yet we still belong to God. God sent Jesus to be our Savior. When we become dirty because of our sins, Jesus cleans us and makes us holy again. When we become broken and worn out, Jesus heals us and makes us whole again. Be glad you belong to God because Jesus is your Savior. He cares about you.

God does not promise that we will have no problems while we live on earth. Billy's toy did get dirty and torn, but Billy cleaned and repaired his toy. We will sin and get into trouble, but God will be with us to help us. When we are hurt, he comforts us. When we are guilty, he forgives us. When we are afraid, he gives us faith and hope.

Be glad that you belong to God. Show your gladness by worshiping him. Think what your life would be like if you did not belong to God. Then thank God that he still claims you and still wants you to be with him. Go to him for help, and worship him all the time.

Let Us Worship God

THE WORD

Come, let us bow down and worship him;
let us kneel before the Lord, our Maker!
He is our God;
we are the people he cares for,
the flock for which he provides.

Psalm 95:6-7a (Christ the King—
Last Sunday after Pentecost)

THE WORLD

Three sheets of paper of the same size and color, cut
a heart from the center of one, a circle from another
and a square from another.

Today's psalm invites us to worship God. It says,
"Come, let us bow down and worship him." We know we
should worship God, but we can't worship him just because we have to. We worship him when we love him,
when we praise and thank him, when we show he is important to us by what we say and do. Our worship is not
real if we do it only because we have to. Our worship
is real when we do it also because we want to.

This psalm helps us want to worship God. It says,
"Let us kneel before the Lord, our Maker! He is our God;
we are the people he cares for, the flock for which he
provides."

We worship God because he is our Maker; he has created us. God did not create us and then forget us. He is
still our God. He provides for us. He takes care of us.
Because God made us and takes care of us, he shows that
he is our God. When we worship him, we show we belong
to him.

Look at it this way: this heart is you *(show paper heart)*. This heart had to be made from something, just as you had to be created. Do you think the heart came from this paper *(show one with square cut from it)?* No, the heart doesn't fit there. Did it come from this *(show paper with circle)?* No, it doesn't belong there. How about this one *(show paper from which heart was cut)?* Look, the heart fits exactly into the hole in this paper. The heart came from this paper, and when it is returned, the paper is complete again.

We need to worship God, because we are always trying to find where we belong. If we worship false gods, we do not fit. The heart cannot go back into the space that is round or square. If we worship money, good grades, people, or any of the other false gods of today, we do not find the place where we fit. Those things did not create us. They do not take care of us.

Sometimes our lives are mixed up because we do not know where we belong. That's why God invites us to worship him. He has invited us to come home again. He is glad he created us. He is glad to take care of us. He enjoys us, and he wants us to enjoy him.

Because our sin has separated us from God, we cannot go back by ourselves. But God still wants us. He sent his Son, Jesus Christ, to be our Savior. Because Jesus is God, he belongs to God. He is a part of this *(show the paper with the heart cut out)*. He helped create us. He is also a part of this *(show the heart)*. He became a part of the creation when he became a person. Now Jesus brings us back to God. Because Jesus is our Savior our lives can be complete again. Now we can worship him.